CHEESES AND THE JUICE
and other
LETTERS

Philip Berry

CHURCH IN THE MARKET PLACE PUBLICATIONS
2014

Church in the Market Place Publications

Cover design by Morag Burton

British Library Cataloguing in Publication Data
A record for this book is available from the British Library

ISBN 978–1–899147–99–1

Typeset in Bookman Old Style
by RefineCatch Ltd, Bungay, Suffolk

Printed in Great Britain by
Cambrian Printers, Aberystwyth

Foreword

It has been a great privilege to encounter Philip's ministry over the past six years since I became Chair of the Chester and Stoke-on-Trent District of the Methodist Church. A significant part of Philip's ministry to people in the chapels across the Dane and Trent Circuit was to write a weekly letter. These 'Letters to a Living Church' were eagerly awaited and became the source of ongoing conversations among the worshipers. Each weekly letter had three parts to it: something drawn from everyday life, a short passage of scripture and a prayer.

What Philip sets up in this book is a dialogue, or conversation, between the reader, everyday life, scripture and prayer. The stories and observations from life help interpret the scripture and the scripture in turn interprets them. So begins in the mind of the reader an engagement with their experiences and the scriptures that feeds prayer. In this way these letters begin to shape a life of discipleship where connections are made between the things that make up daily life and our faith.

I commend this collection of 'letters' to you and pray that it may begin within you a creative engagement between your experiences and the scriptures. The ultimate aim is that we ourselves become living letters in which the events and happenings of life and the stories of our faith recorded in the Bible become interwoven offering 'Living Letters to the World'.

Revd Peter Barber
Methodist Chair of District for Chester & Stoke-on-Trent

Introduction

These 'letters' were never intended to go beyond six weeks, but somehow they kept on appearing. They were never intended for publication. They were just my way of keeping in touch with 19 churches, of which I was Superintendent Minister. Each of them began 'Dear Friends' and ended simply with my name. To avoid what might seem an irritating and endless repetition, these details have been omitted for the purposes of this book.

Those who look for originality will be sorely disappointed. I have gleaned much from the people who have taught me and whose books and writings have helped to shape my journey with Christ. I have frequently turned to them for direction and inspiration.

My other sources for material have been the lives, conversations and stories of those in the Dane and Trent Circuit of the Methodist Church to whom I have been privileged to minister. They know more about Christ than they realise and this book is dedicated to them with much thanks.

Philip Berry
August 2014

A healthy contagion

There are some things that are contagious – and not just diseases. Laughter, hope, faith and love can be contagious, too.

Art thou weary, art thou languid,
Art thou sore distressed?

So runs the old hymn. Was I weary, languid and sore-distressed? Possibly, but not half as much as I was when I was singing about it. Pessimism, judgementalism and despair can be contagious, too.

I prefer instead to sing hymns that draw out of me something deeper. Joy, for a start. When I am joyful I am far better equipped to meet the day. Joy can be contagious, too – and not just the superficial, bubbly, frothy sort either.

Being joyful comes from digging deep down into the heart of our faith. God *is* the kind of God that Jesus has shown him to be. That's the source of Christian joy and it's a contagion that needs spreading.

Singing a new song

Though the fig-tree does not bud, and there are no grapes on the vine,
though the olive crop fails and the fields produce no food,
though there are no sheep in the pen and no cattle in the stalls,
yet will I rejoice in the Lord, I will be joyful in God my Saviour.

Habakkuk 3: 17–18

I have told you this so that my joy may be in you, and that your joy may be complete.

John 15: 11

A Prayer

Lord, why is it that some people who have nothing can act as if they have everything?
I would like some of that unbridled joy.
I thank you for those whose joyfulness makes me glad to be alive.
I thank you for Jesus' joy in you.
Lord, I'm catching it; help me to spread it. Amen

Guardians of the wine

Getting priorities right is never easy. Even today you can still take your life in your hands in certain Methodist circles by mentioning the issue of wine. I have known people get hot under the collar because a glass of wine has appeared at a private garden party (raising money for church funds), or a bottle has been unwittingly donated for the tombola, or even because they have been denied a glass at church to celebrate Grandma's birthday.

Jesus drank wine. He turned water into wine. He offered his life as bread and wine. He made wine more than simply an alcoholic drink to be a symbol for his mission and ministry. And that, to be honest, is rather more important. He challenged people to think of what he was doing as offering new wine that simply could not be contained in old wineskins – be they the institutions of Jesus' day or our own.

As John V. Taylor, a former Bishop of Winchester, once wrote: *we are guardians of the wine, not the skins.* And I think that is the right way to express our priorities. A taste of new wine might do us the power of good.

A parable about new wine

Jesus told them this parable . . . Nor does anyone pour new wine into old wineskins, because the new wine will burst the skins, the wine will pour out and the new wine will be ruined. Instead new wine must be poured into fresh wineskins.

Luke 5: 37

A Prayer

Lord, I must confess it is easier to be a guardian of the skins.
Forgive me when I have mistakenly thought we could contain your Gospel within our church, but I realise you're much bigger than that.
So would you give me also a taste for your new wine?
And if you could still manage to help us keep the skins fresh, I'd like that. Amen

Turning down the jackpot

Have you ever wondered what it would be like to win the Lottery? Never wondered during the sermon what you would do with a million or two? Of course you have. And have you ever imagined what it would be like to meet someone who won the jackpot but then turned it down?

No? What a surprise! But that was what happened to the first disciples the day they met Jesus. This carpenter has the temerity to tell them – and they were experienced fishermen – where to go fishing. In the wrong place, at the wrong time! Against all the odds, Jesus hits the jackpot and the disciples find themselves with the largest haul they have ever had – by some margin.

The fishermen were amazed. Whether that's because of the magnitude of their catch or the fact that Jesus does not seem to want to capitalize on this, I just don't know. But he did not seem interested in benefiting financially. He suggested to the fishermen that there was something more important he had to do, and he wanted them to play a part in it.

We, too, are disciples of a very remarkable Lord – he turns down the jackpot but takes on the Cross.

Having checked the winning numbers . . .

[Simon Peter] *and the others with him were amazed at the large number of fish they had caught. The same was true of Simon's partners, James and John, the sons of Zebedee. Jesus said to Simon, 'Don't be afraid; from now on you will be catching men.'*

Luke 5: 9–10

A Prayer

Lord, I would like to win the Lottery.
You just don't know how generous I could be.
It wouldn't all be for me. Honest.
Well, I can dream, can't I?
If only you hadn't excited those fisherman with better dreams, but you did and they were all the richer for it.
Are those dreams catching? Amen

The vagrant

I heard recently of a Minister who disguised himself – quite effectively – as a rather odorous vagrant who had stumbled into church. He wanted to test how the congregation would welcome such a man. He planned to throw off his disguise at the last moment and reveal who he really was. Unfortunately, the elders called the Police and had him removed before he had a chance!

We pride ourselves on being welcoming; in fact we would hate to think of our congregation as anything but welcoming. What our actions sometimes declare is: *you are welcome – so long as you don't cross the line!*

There are degrees by which people are welcomed. Some we keep at arm's length. Others are fast-tracked into the inner circle. Jesus welcomed sinners; indeed something drew them to him. He spoke with them, but to go to their homes and eat with them was actually an acceptance and welcome of such magnitude that some people could not cope. It was just too unsettling.

Now we would all like a quiet easy life, but the real test of whether we are a welcoming congregation is this: will you welcome the Lord whose will for you might be profoundly unsettling?

Crossing the line

Jesus sat down, called the twelve disciples and said to them: 'Whoever wants to be first must place himself last of all and be the servant of all.' Then he took a child and made him stand in front of them. He put his arms around him and said to them, 'Whoever receives in my name one of these children, welcomes me; and whoever welcomes me, welcomes not only me, but also the one who sent me.'

Mark 9: 35–37

A Prayer

Lord, why is it that welcoming people just isn't as straightforward as I thought? You welcomed people that others didn't rate. I am just glad that you have welcomed me. You had better just help me to welcome you in the same spirit. Amen

Brothers and sisters

Every week two people call me Brother. What they actually say is 'Hi, bro'. I know it sounds slightly cringeworthy, but there is in fact something rather splendid about that. I also ought to add that they are Muslims.

When we call people our brothers and sisters, it changes the way we see them. The early Christian monks of the fourth century did a remarkable thing. They refused to speak of the poor as 'base and ignoble' (as the pagans did), or as 'less fortunate than themselves' (as other Christians did). They called the poor their brothers and sisters. That gave the poor a dignity and respect they had not had before, and it gave the monks a whole new set of friends.

Who are the folk in Mow Cop, Biddulph, and Congleton? In those strange sounding places like Bosley, Harriseahead, Lower Withington or Lask Edge – to name but a few? They are our brothers and sisters in Christ.

At the risk of sounding mischievous, do we sometimes not see one another as 'base and ignoble' or 'less fortunate than ourselves'? Perhaps it would be a bit much if we all went round saying 'Hi, bro' or 'Hi, sis'. But recognizing one another as brothers and sisters is vital to any living church.

Deepening relationships

I have told you this so that my joy may be in you and your joy may be complete. My commandment is this: love one another, just as I love you.

John 15: 11–12

Standing close to the cross were Jesus' mother . . . Jesus saw his mother and the disciple he loved standing there; so he said to his mother, 'He is your son.' Then he said to the disciple, 'She is your mother.'

John 19: 25–27

A Prayer

Lord, I did not choose my brothers and sisters. They came to me as a gift. I would like to say thank you for the gift of my brothers and sisters in [. . .] I thank you for their life of faith, for the skills and gifts I have seen and also those I have failed to notice. Thank you that we share the same calling, the same faith, the same Lord, the same Father. Amen

The fourth of July

July 4th. In some parts of the world you just can't avoid it. July 4th is an occasion for festivities and fireworks as they celebrate their freedom and independence. For Joanna and me it is also the date of our wedding anniversary, when we celebrate going beyond freedom, beyond independence and into what the Bible calls 'covenant'. It is a significant step further – as Joanna would tell you!

Do you remember how long you have been in covenant with God? You might even remember the day you realized that you and God were bound together in love and trust. But do you remember the day, too, when God entered into covenant with you? Well it was long before you were born! To push the analogy further . . . on Good Friday God signed on the dotted line.

Today I ask you to remember just who we are in covenant (relationship) with. God has promised to be our God, and he has gone to extraordinary lengths to keep his promise. You might be tempted at times to think he has forgotten us, and you might then be inclined to settle for as much freedom and independence as you can get. But maybe today, July 4th, he is calling us to go a step beyond that. It is a journey of faith and trust. Don't forget just who it is you are travelling with.

Trusting God

Set your troubled hearts at rest. Trust in God always; trust also in me . . . Thomas said, 'Lord we do not know where you are going, so how can we know the way?' Jesus replied, 'I am the way, the truth and the life; no one comes to the Father except by me.'

John 14: 1, 5–6

A Prayer

Lord, I do wish you had said you could be the way I had always known, the truth I would find easy to come to terms with and the life that suits me. That would be easier. But I guess you don't settle for the easy route. Thank you for waiting for me, trusting me. Help me as I put my trust in you, O Lord. Amen

As small as grasshoppers?

Every now and again I detect a crisis of confidence. *We won't be able to afford this. We won't be able to do that.* Who says? Do beware of self-fulfilling prophecies. If your expectations are set too low, then what you expect might very well happen!

There is an interesting story in Numbers 13–14. The Hebrews, who had recently escaped from Egypt under Moses' leadership, were given a choice. They could either choose to enter the Promised Land, which was 'flowing with milk and honey'. Or they could play it safe, stay in their tents in the desert and eat the manna and quails that God would provide. They chose the tents.

Why? Because although some of the spies who had explored the Promised Land were very taken with its obvious glories, they were scared stiff of the people who lived there and of the hardships and risks involved. As they put it: *We felt as small as grasshoppers.*

Jesus does not call us to be grasshoppers, playing safe and hiding in the grass. *This is a time for spiritual heroes – a time for men and women to be heroic in their faith and in spiritual character and power* [Dallas Willard]. If we expect to make new Christians, God might very well answer more of our prayers than we imagined.

Be bold, be strong / for the Lord your God is with you

Be strong and of good courage. Do not be afraid or dismayed before the King of Assyria and all the horde that is with him; for there is one greater with us than with him.

2 Chronicles 32: 7

A Prayer

Lord, I want to ask you something now, while I feel relatively confident. If the time comes when my confidence is under threat, and I get to feel as small as a grasshopper, well I just ask that you will send me someone who can make me feel different. Someone who can lift me up and restore my faith. Someone who is not content to play things safe. In Jesus' name. Amen

The right person in the right place

If someone were to walk in off the street into your church and say: *I want to learn about being a Christian*, what would you say?

You could make excuses: I am afraid our Minister is not here today. Can you come back in a fortnight? Or you could plead the cause of your own humble limitations: That is not really my forte. But I am sure Mrs S will be able to speak to you. She is so much better at that than I am. You might point out that there is bound to be an Alpha course starting somewhere soon. Just add your name to the list.

Or you could say: You have come just to the right place. The first thing to learn about being a Christian is not to be too fussy about your friends. So, will I do? Put your hand there, son. I have been trying to learn about being a Christian all my life, and I reckon I am just beginning to get the hang of it. Come and sit with me then we'll have a cup of tea.

What we offer in our churches is friendship – in the name of Jesus Christ. The crucial thing is that you and I take responsibility for that – there and then. Finding the right words is nowhere near as important as being the right person in the right place.

From the New Testament

You are the salt of the earth . . . You are the light of the world.

Matthew 5: 13, 14

Do not neglect the gift that is in you . . .

1 Timothy 4: 14

A Prayer

Lord, I have got to thank you for my friends. They are some of the most valuable gifts I have ever received. I would ask you to deepen my capacity for friendship, even when it means I have to live a bit on the edge. Help me to reflect something of your friendship towards me. Amen

Soul whispers

I have enjoyed reading *Prepare for Exile* by Patrick Whitworth. He tells about Monty Roberts who wrote a book called *The Man Who Listens to Horses*. What Roberts discovered was that when wild Mustangs become separated from the herd they actually become sick and even die.

He decided to apply this to breaking in horses. In the ring he decided not to make eye contact with them or even approach them. He reckoned they craved relationships even with their enemy, rather than be ignored and left alone. Instead of spending hours trying to break the horses' wills, this new approach made it possible to get them saddled and with a rider on their back after just one hour.

As we proclaim our faith it does not have to be heavy handed, or confrontational. Sometimes the good news can be whispered through the experience of a loving community, faithful prayers and gentle interest in the lives of others. As Patrick Whitworth puts it, *We need to whisper to people's souls.* Enough perhaps to make people wonder just what it is that makes a Christian tick.

From the Old Testament

Now there was a great wind, so strong that it was splitting mountains and breaking rocks in pieces before the Lord, but the Lord was not in the wind; and after the wind an earthquake, but the Lord was not in the earthquake; and after the earthquake a fire, but the Lord was not in the fire; and after the fire a gentle whisper.

1 Kings 19: 11–12

A Prayer

Breathe through the heats of our desire
Thy coolness and thy balm;
Let sense be dumb, let flesh retire;
Speak through the earthquake, wind and fire
O still small voice of calm.

(From *Dear Lord and Father of mankind*
by John Greenleaf Whittier)

Our Father

Our Father
who art in heaven
hallowed be thy name

No church can be truly alive without prayer. An army marches on its stomach. Christians need to be fed, too. Jesus gave the Lord's Prayer to his disciples when they were hungry. They had seen him praying and asked him to help them pray. He waited till they were hungry enough to ask.

Most of us know the Lord's Prayer by heart. But there may may be occasions when we rattle it off quickly and get to the *Amen* before we realise what we have said. I hope in these next few letters I may encourage you to recapture something of the majesty, the wonder and the power of this remarkable prayer of Jesus.

None of us knows what tomorrow will bring – to our ears, our eyes, our pockets, or our health. We all have to live with a degree of uncertainty. Jesus' disciples knew that only too well. But Jesus did want them to know one thing for certain – that God would remain their Father. No matter what they did, no matter how they behaved, no matter what might unfold, he would remain their Father. That was their starting point.

Our Father *who art in heaven* – well heaven might sound a long way away, but as one wise woman once said, heaven's just a few inches beyond your reach. Close enough for us to be well within God's reach – but not so close that we should think we have him in the palm of our hand. For his name is to be hallowed, kept holy.

A Prayer

Father, I have a lot to do today. But before I get caught up in all of that, I want to start the day with you. Jesus said to call you Father, so I hope I don't sound too presumptuous. I guess that's the one thing I can depend on, the one thing I can be sure about before anything else. Our Father. That's good to know. Amen

The urge to scratch

Thy kingdom come,
Thy will be done
On earth as it is in heaven

If you have got an itch, it's terribly hard not to scratch it. This part of the Lord's Prayer is where Jesus makes people itch, and then positively encourages us to scratch!

Royalty doesn't always get a good press. There may be some kings and queens who are much loved and respected. But, by no means all! Jesus belonged to a people who made it their business to remember a bad king – Pharaoh, the one who had kept them under the yoke of slavery for a long time.

It took Moses' people quite a time to realise that not all kings behaved like that. And when they called God their King, he was nothing like Pharaoh. Quite the opposite, he was a king who wanted to set them free. But it took Jesus, crowned with thorns, to show that some kings might even die for their people.

Jesus makes us itch for something new and different. To pray that God's kingdom might come is to look for, hope and live for a world that lives by radically different 'rules'.

Now those who have the inner strength to resist scratching an itch are in some cases to be admired. But not when you are praying the Lord's Prayer! Once you start saying *Thy will be done* then you are telling God that your resistance is diminishing to the point where you simply have to scratch. Jesus went far beyond saying *Thy will be a good idea*! But God forbid that we should confine such itching to narrowly religious areas. God's will is to be done on earth as well as in heaven.

A Prayer

Lord, when it comes to my horizons,
Lord, when it comes to my faithfulness,
Lord, when it comes to my love for you and for others
bring me up to scratch. Amen

Our daily bread

Give us today our daily bread

What could be more simple or reasonable than that? This is surely the Lord's Prayer at its most down to earth! In fact, it is a radical statement of faith and trust. The language Jesus used takes us back to the 40 years when the people of Israel wandered through the blistering heat of the desert. That is an environment that does not lend itself to producing huge quantities of food. The only thing they could do was trust God. What God then provided was that mysterious manna or bread.

Trusting God does not always come easy, especially when the conditions around us are not exactly what we would like. But that is what Jesus asks us to do – to trust God to give us what we need.

But what exactly does daily bread constitute? A loaf or two? Enough to survive? Enough just for us? Or does it mean bread enough to share, or to give away? Bread enough to whet our appetite for searching for God's will for us? Sometimes we might be tempted to think that God will give us just enough. When Jesus fed the 5,000 there was plenty of bread left over. We must never think of God's love for us as reasonable. It's outrageous!

Now you can't trust in God or his generosity if you then start laying down certain terms and conditions [e.g, I expect everything to be done my way, Lord, as it was in the beginning, etc.]. You have to have your hands and your hearts open.

A Prayer

Guide me, O Thou great Jehovah,
Pilgrim through this barren land.
I am weak, but Thou art mighty;
Hold me with Thy powerful hand.
Bread of heaven, bread of heaven,
Feed me till I want no more;
Feed me till I want no more.
(by William Williams)

Forgiveness or probation

And forgive us our trespasses
As we forgive those that trespass against us

When the people of Israel, under Moses, crossed the Red Sea it was a major step forward. They crossed a barrier which had breadth and depth and which had seemed insurmountable.

Forgiveness, as far as Jesus was concerned, meant crossing a barrier just as broad and just as deep – and just as significant.

Try not to pray this part of the Lord's Prayer too quickly. (It took a while to cross the Red Sea.) Asking God to forgive you may not be that hard. Accepting his forgiveness might be something else. There is just as much an art to receiving as there is to giving.

Forgiving other people, well that seems to be a fundamental part of Jesus' way of living. Sometimes we think we are forgiving people when all we are actually doing is putting them on probation. We'll let bygones be bygones, providing . . . Whether people will always accept the offer of forgiveness is a different matter, but don't think this is an easy thing. It is not.

In this part of the Lord's Prayer, Jesus teaches us to receive a precious gift. He also encourages us to let go of the bitterness, resentments, fears and animosities that we can so easily harbour and nurture, and which can be so destructive.

A Prayer

Lord, it is not easy for me to accept anything. I have my pride and my independence. It is not easy for me to accept forgiveness – from you or anybody else. I don't like to think I may have got things wrong. But I guess I have – often. Thank you for not condemning me or holding me to account. You need to know I am not as good at forgiving as you, so I am going to need a little help. Especially with you know who. Amen

Take care you don't step backwards

Lead us not into temptation
But deliver us from evil.

Every now and again, in our churches, there comes a sudden spark of clarity, a breath of inspiration, a sense of excitement and hope. This is when people begin to dream, anticipate and imagine a new kind of future. It is often the point when we are truly listening to God.

Then we take stock, we think of all this would cost, how difficult things would be. We think of all the obstacles that would need to be surmounted. And we start thinking of all the reasons why we should stay exactly where we are. And before you know where we are, we have taken a step back.

Jesus asked us not to be led into temptation for the very good reason that he knew we would be. He also asked for us to be delivered. Some people think of evil as something or someone out there. [You can always tell, you know!?] I think, though, that evil is anything (out there or inside us) that threatens to diminish or crush our spirits.

When that spark of clarity is allowed to flourish, when the breath of inspiration can he held and cherished, when the sense of excitement can be welcomed and shared, then maybe the deliverance for which we long is not so far away.

A Prayer

Lord, I am not certain whether I am going forwards or backwards. I know what suits me, but there is that part of me which longs deep down to do your will. If I get tempted to go backwards, could you just find a way of letting me know? And where there is truly a movement of your Spirit, count me in. Amen

I'd just like a little word with you

Most of us enjoy a good chat, whether it takes the form of casual conversation, reminiscences of the past, discussion of what's going on around us – and even, come to think of it, a good argument or gossip.

It's probably those very normal experiences that have most informed the way we think and act, or even changed the way we have seen other people and the world. Not surprising then that God has given us the gift of prayer. And if you do that regularly enough you find that you are not just dropping in for a chat with God, he is also dropping in for a chat with you.

Relationships – with one another and with God – are important. There is always a temptation to think that other remedies are going to work. If there is a political threat, just send in more military power. If people are getting ill or old, just throw in a few more technological aids and devices. If people are lonely, well there is always retail therapy to call on.

But in the end there is no substitute for good relationships. That's what we are designed for. That's also what God wants with us. Mind you, when someone says, *I'd just like a little word with you*, you are never quite sure what you are in for.

What happens when Jesus drops in for a chat?

A certain man [at the healing pool in Jerusalem] had been infirm for 38 years. Jesus said to him, 'Do you want to get well?' The sick man answered, 'Sir, I have no-one to put me in the pool when the water is stirred; while I am trying to get there another person gets in front of me!' Jesus said to him, 'Rise, take up your pallet and walk.' And at once the man was cured . . . Afterwards Jesus found him in the Temple and said to him, 'Behold, you are cured. Sin no more . . .'

John 5: 1–15

A Prayer

Lord, you do that, don't you? Drop in for a chat when I am doing something else, when I am busy. It's a bit unsettling, you know. Couldn't you give me a bit of notice? Forewarned is forearmed, you know. Lord, why do I sometimes feel you have a big smile on your face? Amen

It takes your breath away

One of the things that sometimes staggers me is how our churches and chapels ever got to be built in the first place. A small group of people perhaps met together for a while in someone's house and then had the vision and the determination to build something more permanent – sometimes it would seem in the most unlikely of places.

Why would they do that? Well no doubt we could dig up a variety of mixed motives, but this is not a time to waste on cynicism. I suspect that behind that zeal and enterprise lies the simple truth that a number of people had had their breath taken away by the sound of the Christian gospel.

There are all sorts of things that can take our breath away, from the beauty – or the horror – of the scene in front of us, to some unexpected surprise or the way some people have responded (in generosity, faith or courage) to what life has presented them with. Indeed, in the end, life is not measured by the number of breaths we take but by the moments that took our breath away!

Remember that Jesus touched – and still does – people's lives. In what he said and did. What takes my breath away is that this was not just for people 2,000 years ago, or even for 'them out there'. It was for me, even me!

After Jesus healed a paralysed man

While they all watched, the man got up, picked up his mat, and hurried away. They were all completely amazed and praised God saying, 'We have never seen anything like this.'

Mark 2: 12

A Prayer

Amazing grace (how sweet the sound)
That saved a wretch like me!
I once was lost, but now am found,
Was blind, but now I see.

(by John Newton)

The lure of raisin cakes

Long ago, in my formative years, an old local preacher knelt down in front of our family in his sitting room and, quite spontaneously, prayed for us. It was, to an awkward teenager, both embarrassing and yet moving at the same time and I have never forgotten that occasion.

Well it might be a trifle embarrassing but let me remind you that, when push comes to shove, we exist as Christian congregations because of God's commitment to us. And our Gospel is that God did a lot more than get on his knees.

This week and next, I want to point out three ways the Old Testament uses to express that awareness of God's commitment. First of all he *loves*. Doesn't sound much on the face of it. But there is a lovely line in Hosea (3: 1) that speaks of God loving his people even when they turn to other gods and love raisin cakes!

You can't get more down to earth than that. Whether it's big things (gods) or little things (raisin cakes) that appeal to our senses and appetites and get in the way of our loving God, God is still committed to us in a big way. And that is at the heart of costly love. And that is a love that will stay with us.

I have loved you with an everlasting love;
therefore I have continued my faithfulness to you.
Jeremiah 31: 3

A Prayer

Lord, I love raisin cakes, lemon meringue pies, creature comforts and a settled life, but you raise love to an altogether higher plane, and give it a broader, deeper dimension. I hope I am fairly committed, but could you let some of that richer vein of commitment rub off on me? Like it did in Jesus. Amen

The Lord chose *you*

Last week I wrote of *love* as one of the ways the Old Testament uses to express God's commitment to his people. Now let me turn to two others.

First, God *chooses*. The people of Israel emerge as his chosen people. Now frankly we find that a little embarrassing. Why should one group of people be singled out as more special than another? The strange thing was that the people of Israel did not find it embarrassing at all. They rather relished the idea, and also became aware of the responsibilities that carried. It did not mean that God loved everyone else the less! Jesus, too, picked up on the idea and told his disciples they were to pick up that calling of a chosen people and make a difference – as the salt of the earth and light for the world. Quite a thought that God chooses us to be the bearers of his Gospel. There's foolhardy commitment for you.

Second, God *sets his heart* on his people. This is God not just being foolhardy. This is God in all his passionate commitment.

From the Old Testament

For you are a people holy to the Lord your God; the Lord your God has chosen you out of all the people on earth to be his people, his treasured possession. It was not because you were more numerous than any other people that the Lord set his heart on you and chose you – for you were the fewest of all peoples. It was because the Lord loved you and kept the oath that he swore to your ancestors.

Deuteronomy 7: 6–8

A Prayer

Lord, sometimes we feel it, you know. There are not many of us, and none of us are getting any younger. Yet that conviction that you want us, have chosen us, to help fulfil your purposes won't go away. Thank you for that. Thank you for setting your heart on us. Thank you for being passionate about us. Amen

Love is all it takes

Loving God, serving Christ, loving people – whatever it takes

That's what is being proposed as the strapline for a new Circuit Mission statement. Now such things are usually consigned to the back of the drawer of one's consciousness as soon as they have been printed. But before you do that, just look at what it is saying.

There are lots of things in life that are complicated – from international diplomacy, astrophysics, cracking the human genome code, to deciphering the instructions for assembling flat-pack furniture.

But God is not really complicated. Not like those sorts of things and not like people, either. They are certainly complicated. Always, we have to gauge and judge whether people are trustworthy, reliable and genuine, and whether following them or listening to them is going to make matters better or worse.

God is not complicated. He is just in love with us. And not just us, but all kinds of people that we probably think are inherently unlovable! He even sends his son to push the boundaries of his love. And, if the Cross says anything at all, he is a God who is prepared to do whatever it takes to love us. A God like that is remarkable, to say the least, but he is not complicated.

My thoughts are not your thoughts, nor are your ways my ways, says the Lord.

Isaiah 55: 8

A Prayer

Lord, I get the impression from Jesus that we are always at the front of your thoughts, so it seems a bit odd that you are often at the back of mine. I wish that wasn't the case, but that's the truth. I know my ways are not like your ways, so I will have to trust your love to bridge the gap. Amen

The one thing I lack

Loving God*, serving Christ, loving people – whatever it takes*

My daughter is now in Australia. That's what she wanted to do; and I encouraged her to go. We talk regularly on the phone – usually at my expense – and every now and again we Skype. That means you can see and talk to one another through your computers, and it doesn't cost a penny. Sometimes loving people is a costly business, and sometimes it isn't. And those you love – well, you go on loving them whether you can see them or not.

One of the things we try to do as Christians is to love God. Sometimes that means letting God be himself, go where he chooses, be the kind of God he is (rather than the Lord High Protector of my Private Interests) and being glad about it.

But there is another thing about loving God. You sometimes have to be prepared to take risks. You have to be prepared to lose some things to find something more important. You can't love God when you are wrapped in a security blanket. It means trusting him – rather than yourself or your possessions. It helps if you talk regularly, though there is always a chance that that might change you, your priorities, or the way you see things.

A reminder that loving God can be demanding

Jesus said: There is still one thing you lack: sell everything you have and give to the poor, and you will have treasure in heaven; then come and follow me.

Luke 18: 22

A Prayer

Lord, whatever you do, don't tell me the one thing I lack. Tell me you could do with a little help here and there, but don't tell me what I lack. Or if you do, don't suggest what I might do about it, because I am 99.9% certain it would not be what I would choose ... What was that Lord? The Lord is my shepherd; therefore I shall lack nothing! Make that 100%. Amen

The critical moment

Loving God, ***serving Christ****, loving people – whatever it takes*

Today, a man is asking you something. He once walked along the shores of a distant lake. He once called people to leave their homes and their jobs, even their responsibilities, not because they were not important – they were – but because this was the critical moment in their lives on which all else depended.

This man died and rose again. That simple remarkable statement of faith carries with it the critical and good news on which Christian faith stands: He is the risen Lord.

It is Christ Jesus who is speaking to you, asking you to serve him. He does not ask you about your qualifications, or your age, or your experience or where you come from. He simply asks you to serve him. He knows you want to serve your family, your friends, your town, your church. But he calls you to serve him – as a priority.

And now he is asking you how you are going to serve him today. How you answer him may be a critical moment not just for you, but for all of us.

Serving Christ

. . . and he died for all, that those who live might no longer live for themselves but for him who for their sake died and was raised.

2 Corinthians 5: 15

A Prayer

Lord, it's a frightening thought that so much depends on how we respond at the critical moments in our lives. What amazes me is how you got it right, time after time, even when others were pushing you to take a different course. Help me to recognise the critical moment when it comes, and guide me then to act as the servant you have called me to be. Amen

Why so much?

Loving God, serving Christ, ***loving people*** *– whatever it takes*

The Gospels tell the story of Jesus and in the background there are some very significant people who are an important part of that story. Some of them are named – blind Bartimaeus, for example, or the disciples – Peter, James and John. Then there was Mary, the mother of Jesus and Mary Magdalene. Some are given little more than a title – a rich young man, a centurion – by which they can be identified.

Beyond that there were the crowds who are sometimes mentioned following Jesus around. Occasionally they are even fed in their thousands. They witness what Jesus did; listen in to the stories he told; they welcome him into the city of Jerusalem; and ultimately have a profound say in the outcome of the trials he faces.

Jesus loved people – children, women, rich, poor, soldiers, sinners. He gave them a sense of what they were worth to God. Which was a lot more than some people thought. But then that was part of the scandal of the Gospel, and Jesus paid for that with his life.

When we really fulfil our calling to love people, it will not simply result in them feeling they are of value, it will also leave others asking the question: why so much?

From Matthew's Gospel

. . . when I was hungry, you gave me food; when thirsty, you gave me a drink; when I was a stranger, you took me into your home; when naked, you clothed me; when I was ill, you came to my help; when in prison, you visited me.

Matthew 25: 35–36

A Prayer

Lord, *love* is a much easier word to say than to put into practice. But I suppose you already know that. You talked about going the extra mile, giving two shirts away when only one was asked for. I am going to need your help loving people, especially when you want me to push out the boundaries like you did. Fair dos? Amen

The hoovering of the Temple

Loving God, serving Christ, loving people – ***whatever it takes***

There is a really clever advertisement going around for Dyson vacuum cleaners. What Dyson says they are about is this: *Solve the obvious problems – whatever it takes.* I rather like that. And, of course, *whatever it takes* is usually rather more than you might expect.

Now it is true that vacuum cleaners do not figure much in the New Testament, but that momentous last week of Jesus' life did begin with a clean-up operation. Jesus created quite a stir – more than enough for the disciples, thank you very much – as he drove out of the Temple those who had had the temerity to rip people off in the name of God. But Jesus was not finished there. The problems his people faced were not all obvious; they were deep-rooted, and a once-over with the vacuum cleaner was never going to be enough. He was determined to do whatever it took to fulfil his people's calling. And the measure of that is the Cross.

Now we have some obvious problems to solve in our Circuit if we are to fulfil our calling and have a viable future. And we have some less obvious problems, too. If we are really going to address them as faithful followers of Jesus Christ, we will have to do whatever it takes. That's not easy; indeed it will demand a great deal of us in loving God, serving Christ and loving others.

Must go. Got to get the vacuum cleaner out.

On doing whatever it takes

'I will follow you, sir, but let me first say goodbye to my people at home.' To him Jesus said, 'No-one who sets his hand to the plough and then looks back is fit for the kingdom of God.'

Luke 9: 61–62

A Prayer

Lord, I sometimes think you would have been wiser to have hoovered the Temple rather than cleansed it. But then your ways are not my ways! I pray for my little temple today and all the people who are a part of it. Cleanse us, so that we really can serve the purposes you intend. I hesitate to say it, but do whatever it takes. Amen

River crossings

We have just been on our travels and they took us to the north-east. We seemed to cross rivers with great regularity – the Wansbeck, Aln and Tyne to name just a few. Some we were aware of, while others just passed unnoticed beneath us. Yet crossing a river at one time was a major event. Whether there happened to be a bridge or a ford or a boat, you knew about it.

Jesus took crossing a river as a highly significant moment. This was where you moved into new, uncharted territory. Going back might not be so simple. Mark 10 tells how Jesus was crossing the River Jordan when James and John asked for the two key positions in his 'new administration'. They were probably crossing a ford – not too difficult. But Jesus made it clear that where they were heading was going to take them into much deeper water. They would almost certainly lose their lives.

The real question was not whether James and John could have key appointments. It was whether they were really prepared to go with Jesus. And Jesus crossed the Jordan trusting that whatever he faced God would be with him.

The Dane and Trent Circuit takes its name from two rivers. That could mean we are content to live within certain (safe) boundaries or it could mean we are the kind of people who, in the name of Jesus, are prepared to cross rivers when that is what needs to be done.

It all began at a river

It was at this time that Jesus came from Nazareth in Galilee and was baptized in the Jordan by John. As he was coming up out of the water, he saw the heavens break open and the Spirit descend upon him, like a dove. And a voice came from heaven: You are my beloved Son; in you I take delight.

Mark 1: 9–11

A Prayer

Lord, right now I am not exactly certain what river you want me to cross and where to do so. But when the time comes, give me the courage and the humility to cross over it as one of your servants. You tell me it will be hard but good on the other side. You will have to put up with my struggles to believe it. Thanks for the oars by the way. Amen

St Mary's lighthouse

I have always had a fascination with lighthouses. Their simple yet elegant design, and the backdrop of raw and inspiring seascapes and landscapes is quite a combination. One of my earliest memories is of visiting St Mary's Lighthouse just north of Whitley Bay. After a gap of over 50 years I recently paid my second visit.

St Mary's was built in 1898 to replace the one at Tynemouth Castle. Unfortunately that had become obscured by pollution from the Tyne's industry as well as by passing shipping. That earlier lighthouse at Tynemouth Castle had a long and distinguished history. In the twelfth century, monks kept a light burning in the church tower on the headland (and in their priory on St Mary's Island). When the priory at Tynemouth Castle fell into disrepair in the seventeenth century, a 79-foot tower was built from stone from the ruins. The light from a coal fire at the top would have saved many lives.

St Mary's was a working lighthouse the first time I was there, powered by paraffin vapour. In between my visits, they switched to electricity. Then it was automated. Now it is discontinued. The light has simply moved on.

Jesus said, *I am the light of the world.* If we are a living church we position the light where it can best be seen, and where it can do the job God intended it to do.

From the New Testament

And the light shines on in the darkness, and the darkness has never put it out.

John 1: 5

A Prayer

Lord, I want to thank you for all the churches of our Circuit, for the way the light of Christ has been kept alive and for all that that has meant to so many over the years. Give us today the vision and courage to focus the light where you want it to shine, and to walk the path you light up for us. Amen

Saints to be treasured

The north-east is almost awash with saints. Years ago when I was at University, I went to St Chad's College in Durham. I never gave a second thought as to who St Chad was. Mind you, he never asked about me either.

Just a trip to Holy Island brings you almost face to face with the life and legacy of two of our country's finest – St Aidan, arguably the greatest evangelist we have ever had, and St Cuthbert, former Bishop of Lindisfarne and the 'reason' behind Durham Cathedral. At least that is where he was buried. They also gave their names to Durham colleges.

Now I have to say that even when you take away all the legends and stories that accrue around the saints, they still stand as remarkable characters whose lives and love of Christ sometimes render you speechless. These guys were extraordinary. They had that capacity to stop people in their tracks and make them look at life in new ways.

Now there's no shortage of saints in Cheshire and Staffordshire either – and some of them are still living. They are to be found in all our churches. There is no need to venerate them but do treasure them, and ask what it is that makes them the people they are. The one thing that will unite them is not that they have grasped hold of the Christian gospel. It's rather that something of the Christian Gospel has grasped hold of them and they have said *Yes, Amen.*

A reminder of what we are called to be

To the church of God which is at Corinth, to those who are sanctified in Christ Jesus, called to be saints, with all who in every place call on the name of Jesus Christ our Lord, both theirs and ours: grace to you and peace from God our Father and the Lord Jesus Christ.

1 Corinthians 1: 2–3

A Prayer

Lord, what do you mean you want me to be a saint? Can't you just accept me as I am, warts and all, and be done with it? Besides which, I think by and large sinners have a better time! If you insist on working with raw material, that's up to you. I will follow you. I will call on you. But frankly, I think you have got your work cut out. Amen

Getting well connected

What have Pig's Nose Pippin, Jazz, Zari and Reverend W. Wilks got in common? Yes, you are quite right, they are varieties of apple. That was just one of the inconsequential details that hit me as I toured the greenhouses of one of Victorian England's greatest houses and gardens (Cragside) in the north-east.

Now just what do you have to do to give your name to an apple? I am not exactly certain who Pig's Nose Pippin was but he may simply have had an unforgettable face. As for the Reverend W. Wilks, was he a saint, perhaps the revered parish priest or an avid gardener? Possibly, but his position as secretary of the Royal Horticultural Society at the beginning of the twentieth century may also have had something to do with it.

Cragside showed me there were more varieties of apples than I had previously thought. They came in all shapes and sizes, too. It also struck me that one of things Jesus asked us to do was to bear fruit. It would be silly to limit the ways in which we do that – God did not command us to be all the same, any more than he commanded there to be one variety of apple – but that we do bear fruit is an essential characteristic of any living church.

And to bear fruit – whatever your name is – you need to be well connected. Not to the Royal Horticultural Society, but to the living Lord.

As Jesus put it:

This is how my father is glorified: you are to bear fruit in plenty and so be my disciples.

John 15: 8

A Prayer

Lord, you don't do things by halves do you? You don't just want a little bit of fruit, a token apple or orange here and there. You want fruit by the basket load, plenty of it, you said. That in all honesty is a bit frightening, almost overwhelming, and if you want us to bear more fruit then maybe we could do with a change in climate. And while we are on the subject, a bit more sunshine wouldn't go amiss either, Lord. Amen

Tomorrow shall be my dancing day

Up and down the country in the entrance halls and meeting rooms of churches, after services and sometimes before, an animated discussion is taking place. There is a sense of expectation and excitement in the air. The Advent season is upon us and you can feel the tension build up with each passing week. What will happen next? The waiting is unbearable. Will Ann Widdecombe really win *Strictly Come Dancing*? And thank God those who have been voting for so-and-so on *The X Factor* have had their phone lines disconnected.

In trying times – and we have had a few – the need for welcome diversions is ever greater. The scene is set for a new star to emerge. A new king (or queen) will be crowned. There are even three wise men in attendance. [I am not sure that Craig Greville Horwood and Louis Walsh qualify.]

In between these discussions, Advent services are taking place. They could be the religious equivalents of such seasonal entertainment and indeed a welcome diversion, laced as they often are with nostalgia, tradition and – in the main – good spirits. But, if we get those services right they do far more than that. They will tell a story, which many may choose to write off as a children's winter tale, but, strictly speaking, points at a deeper truth: that God is not just with us in a vague sense, but in that unique life of Jesus he has thrown all his eggs into one (Moses) basket. He has voted for us, and that makes the winner this year . . . us!

From an old English Carol

Tomorrow shall be my dancing day;
I would my true love did so chance
To see the legend of my play,
To call my true love to my dance;
    Sing, oh! my love, oh! my love, my love, my love,
    This have I done for my true love.

A Prayer

Lord, if I don't seem quite as interested in your story as *Strictly* or *The X Factor*, that's only because I know how your story ends . . . Sorry, you mean it hasn't ended yet? You want me to dance, to come forward with my gifts? No, I'm running ahead with myself. I guess you just want me for the moment to watch you dance. Well, I'm watching you, Lord. Your dancing day is coming and I'm watching. Amen

John the Baptist

The first church where I was appointed the Minister was a Methodist–Baptist Church. It was unusual in that it became one of the few Methodist Churches in the country that had a pool installed for the baptism of believers (as opposed to children) by total immersion. Some of you will remember heating elements that you could plug into the car's lighter socket and heat up some soup or coffee. This pool was heated by a giant version of those. It was plugged in for 17 hours at a time and on a good day the temperature could rise to being positively tepid. Sadly, one lady tripped over the edge one year and caused quite an injury to her leg when she fell in.

One of the characters we come across in Advent is John the Baptist. He asked people to prepare for the coming of the Lord by repentance, by baptism. [I can feel your excitement levels almost at the tepid level now!] That means he was asking individuals to be different. Not for the sake of being different, but because the coming of the Messiah was such a significant event that really you could do no other.

Sometimes we are encouraged to believe that people can't be different. Sometimes people don't even think they can be different. And that is exactly why John the Baptist keeps cropping up every Advent. He thought they could be different.

Incidentally, the choir had to move to a new place in that church – no small decision – to accommodate the baptistery. I think they sang better afterwards, too. Christ is coming. Can you and I accommodate John the Baptist? Just watch where you put your feet.

From the New Testament

The beginning of the good news of Jesus Christ, the Son of God . . .

'See, I am sending my messenger ahead of you, who will prepare your way; the voice of one crying in the wilderness: Prepare the way of the Lord . . .'

Mark 1: 1–3

A Prayer

Lord, this Advent, I want to repent. I want to walk the way of the Lord without being diverted up dead ends and cul-de-sacs. As Bethlehem gets nearer, help me get nearer to you. And give me the courage to walk the way you prepare today. Amen

The penny and the orange

Every year as a child I found at the bottom of my pillowcase the same two presents. They were a brand new penny and an orange. They were the least valuable and yet the most remembered of all my presents. After a couple of years or so, you started looking for them.

I don't know what was in my parents' thinking at the time, but I would like to think they wanted me to learn that any gift, no matter how small, was something to be treasured and valued. While I, my brother and sisters, all had different presents, these were the ones that united us, that showed we were equally loved.

Gifts of course figure in the Christmas story. Strangely enough, people seem to have no difficulty remembering the expensive gifts – gold, frankincense and myrrh – even if they haven't the foggiest idea what at least two of them were. The most important gift though was this child who was to express more of the currency of God's love than anyone had ever seen.

At Christmas, perhaps more than any other time, we have to practise the art of receiving. Jesus is nothing less than God's gift of himself and it's worth delving to the bottom of Christmas to look for him. At the very least you may begin to understand a bit more about our Father.

The Word became flesh and lived among us, and we have seen his glory.
John 1: 14

A Prayer

Lord, I don't pretend to understand everything about the mystery of Christmas. But I think I have got this right – that you have pitched your tent in my back garden, if you don't mind me referring to Bethlehem in that way. I have a penny, but if I owned the world I could never repay you that gift. I have an orange, but I don't think even that measures up to your gift of yourself. Amen

Swaddled, the shepherds' way

My favourite characters in the Christmas story are the shepherds. It is their experience that gives us an insight into the kind of God we are dealing with. They were largely poor, uneducated people, who frankly did not count for a lot. Certainly not the kind of characters you give special invitations to willy-nilly.

They were spoken to by angels first and they were afraid. And who wouldn't be? You would think your number was up, wouldn't you? A group of shepherds turning up out of the blue at Bethlehem then would likely be given much the same shrift as at Macclesfield Hospital Maternity Unit today. Their fears were allayed only when they realized they would find the child wrapped in swaddling clothes – the peasant way, just like theirs – and laid in a manger. Mangers were often inside peasant houses, and the (surprising) news that the infant Jesus was to be born in a house just like one of theirs no doubt spurred them on.

The shepherds left praising God for all that they had seen or heard. There is no need to think that the conditions at the house were wretched just because they were poor. If they had been, you would have expected them to offer something better.

Like shepherds, there is a time for us too to conquer our fears. And it is probably best not to try and second-guess God. This is a day for listening to angels.

And suddenly there was with the angel a multitude of the heavenly host praising God and saying: 'Glory to God in the highest heaven and on earth peace among those whom he favours.'

Luke 2: 13–14

A Prayer

Lord, you are the God of the highest heaven and your son gets born in an ordinary house! Thank you for making ordinary people like shepherds partners in your purposes. Thank you for welcoming them, and sharing the hospitality of people like them. Thank you for allowing me to celebrate Christmas with you. Amen

New Year

Let me begin the New Year by introducing you to the wise men. Tradition says they were called Melchior, Caspar and Balthasar, but who knows? The Bible does not even tell us how many there were. And of course they followed a star.

If you read Isaiah 60, you will find the prophet dreaming of the wonderful things that would happen in Jerusalem:

> Arise, shine for your light has come and the glory of the Lord has risen upon you . . . The wealthy of the nations shall come to you . . . They shall bring gold and frankincense and shall proclaim the praise of the Lord.

That dream was never fulfilled. But Matthew felt that those dreams and expectations were not dead. But instead of seeing them focused on a place (Jerusalem), he believed that they had now landed on the child born at Bethlehem. The glory of the Lord shone on Jesus, not on those ancient walls. And the wise men/kings visited a child, not a city.

The temptation today is always to transfer that glory back again onto a place (our church), but if we are wise men and women we will recognise that our churches achieve their highest glory when they point in word and action to Christ, the light of the world.

A Christmas hymn

Hark! the herald angels sing
Glory to the new-born King.

A Prayer

Lord, it's a new year and here I am again. I don't know whether I am any different from this time last year, but I trust you are still as forgiving. I would like this to be a great year for my family and friends, for my church and for those I work with. If it isn't, I daresay you and I will have words, but I am sure you can cope with that. Give me the wisdom to get my priorities right, and like the wise men to go back by another route when I get things wrong. Amen

The Authorized Version

In 1610 a remarkable meeting took place in London at Abergavenny House, which stood on the site of the current Stationers Hall. To call it one meeting would be something of a distortion for the 12 men who attended actually met every day for 9 months. They came to put together the final touches and amendments to the new translation of a Bible in English, the King James Version. It was to be published in 1611, 400 years ago, an achievement that will be marked by celebrations across the country over the course of the next 12 months.

The 12 probably included representatives of the six 'companies' of over 50 scholars who had combined their expertise in the ancient languages of the Bible – Hebrew, Greek, Aramaic, Syriac, Latin – and in the modern languages into which the Bible had already been translated – Spanish, Italian, German, French – to produce a version of the Bible in English that could command both common approval and widespread availability.

The King James Version of 1611, or the Authorized Version as it is sometimes called, was a remarkable feat of scholarship. But it was never intended to be a version just for scholars. It was meant to read well when it was spoken either in church or at home. And you should hear what God put into it. Really, you should. It doesn't matter much which version you use today. God still wants to speak to you through it.

The risen Lord meets two disciples on the way to Emmaus

And beginning with Moses and all the Prophets, he explained to them what was said in all the Scriptures concerning himself . . . They asked each other, 'Were not our hearts burning within us while he talked with us on the road and opened the Scriptures to us?'

Luke 24: 27, 32

A Prayer

Lord, sometimes as I don't read the Bible as much as I should because I am afraid I won't understand it, King James might have authorized some scholars to guide me through it. But he didn't. So Lord, if I am going to know your book better, I hope you will make it come alive for me. For Jesus' sake. Amen

An eccentric at work

I recently heard of an American man who is writing the Bible out long-hand on carefully lined paper and with indelible ink. He got the idea from his partner, a Muslim, with whom he has been living for 20 years. It's not that uncommon apparently in Islamic tradition to write the Koran out by hand.

You might think it is a bit over the top, but he is driven by a desire to understand what is in the Bible. Listening to a verse here and a chapter there, he says, means we know the Bible in pieces but not as a whole. He wanted to see the big picture and encourage others to do the same. He frequently reads sections of the Bible aloud before putting them to paper.

Philip Patterson used to be an interior decorator but, since he has had AIDS for the past 24 years, he has not been able to work. He wanted to find something useful to do with his time that was within his limitations. He has been at it now for several years, patiently writing out page after page in his beautiful swirling script.

Maybe writing down by hand passages you have read and enjoyed is not as daft as it sounds. I would not recommend the whole Bible personally, but to see hand-written pages that others have come to love and appreciate displayed in our churches might be quite interesting to see, read and digest.

From the Old Testament

But this is the covenant that I will make with the house of Israel after those days, says the Lord: I will put my law within them, and I will write it on their hearts; and I will be their God, and they shall be my people.

Jeremiah 31: 33

A Prayer

Lord, it strikes me that you call a lot of eccentric people to be Christians, and it also strikes me that they are not all in America, not by a long way. I pray for all my eccentric friends in our churches and I pray that we may all learn how to use our eccentricities to spread the gospel of forgiving and renewing grace that we have found in Christ. Amen

Boris and the Bible

Boris Johnson is an interesting character. That is partly explained by the language that he uses. 'Crack on' is not a phrase we hear very often. And I don't suppose many of us had heard of the term 'wiff waff' for table-tennis till he came out with it. [Incidentally Wiff Waff was the name given to a game that titled folks would play 300 years ago on large dinner tables using cigar box lids as paddles and a cork as the object. The paddle and cork would come together making a wiff-waff sound. It was indeed the precursor of table-tennis.] It's an old-fashioned language that Boris speaks that perhaps reflects his social background.

Now I mention that because it is a common misconception that the King James Bible was the Good News Bible of its day. We assume people said *thee, thou, doth, saith, makest,* etc. as their normal speech in the early seventeenth century. Only they didn't. Language was already changing and the King James was written in a rather archaic tone even then. The translators were partly, I suspect, early versions of Boris who spoke a different English to the common man. They also wanted to use the language that had already been used to good effect in the earlier English versions of the Bible over the previous 100 years.

Whether you find the language of the King James Version easy to read or not, it did carry with it even in 1611 a sense that you were listening to something special and unique – that this was the word of God. Sorry if I have interrupted your reading the Bible. Crack on.

From the New Testament [King James Version]

Our Father which art in heaven,
Hallowed be Thy name.
Thy kingdom come.
Thy will be done on earth, as it is in heaven.
Give us this day our daily bread.
And forgive us our debts, as we forgive our debtors.
And lead us not into temptation, but deliver us from evil:
For thine is the kingdom, and the power, and the glory, for ever.
Amen

Matthew 6: 9–13

A bit of mischief

There was a bit of a hoohah in 1631 when the latest edition of the King James Version (KJV) was printed. There were a couple of unfortunate printer's errors which resulted in most of the offending 'Wicked Bibles' being destroyed. Suffice it to say that if you have a KJV that says *Thou shalt commit adultery* it's probably worth a bob or two! Nor was this the only error. Deuteronomy 5: 24 read: *the Lord our God hath shewed us his glory and his great asse* (instead of greatnesse). Seventeenth-century English would probably have seen *ass* as a very respectable word for *donkey*, rather than its more modern meaning, but this was still bordering on the blasphemous.

The cause of all this may well lie in disputes between various printers as to who had the printing rights and the whole affair has sabotage written all over it. Which all goes to show that even those who hold the Bible dear are still capable of a bit of mischief when it suits them.

This year our Circuit needs to find creative ways in which we play to our strengths and become not only more viable but also more effective witnesses to the Gospel of Jesus Christ. Fears, old grudges or a desire for the comfort of a much loved familiarity may tempt us into burying our heads in the sand or even putting spokes in the wheel. And that would be a bit of mischief we could well do without.

From the letters of St Paul in the New Testament

I therefore, the prisoner in the Lord, beg you to lead a life worthy of the calling to which you have been called, with all humility and gentleness, with patience, bearing with one another in love, making every effort to maintain the unity of the Spirit in the bond of peace.

Ephesians 4: 1–3

A Prayer of Confession

Lord, you know me better than I know myself and you know that I can be as capable of mischief as anyone else. There are times when it is fun, and there are times when I even think I am doing the right thing. But not always. Forgive the mischief in me that hurts and stands in the way of your gospel. Amen

Rough Music

There was a practice is the nineteenth century in this country called 'Rough Music'. If you felt the law was not going to be much help to you, or the police were hamstrung, you could get a number of people to help you deal with the upstarts who had offended you. Basically you met at night outside their home with as many people as you could muster and subjected them to three nights or so of deafening noise. Pots, tins, shovels, horns, rattles and drums were beaten incessantly. You could apply this to anyone who had committed adultery, beaten their wife, re-married with indecent haste, hen-pecked their husband or who had in some other way got the backs up of their town or village. The police usually made themselves scarce.

What a good idea, you might say, but the potential for abuse was in fact pretty horrific. 'Rough music' was just a noisy form of mob rule and those that took part may have been no better than the hapless 'victims'. Those who took pleasure in being vindictive or who were easily swayed by spite, gossip, or rumour would have had a field day.

The fact is that in life, people, even other Christians sometimes, do rub you up the wrong way. You can respond with some twenty-first century form of 'rough music' or you can sing a different tune. When Jesus was confronted with difficult people and situations he often turned to the Psalms. Over the next three weeks, I would like to point out one or two things about the Psalms. It will be little more than a rough guide. But the Psalms have lasted rather longer than 'Rough Music' did and need to be appreciated.

From Psalm 137

By the rivers of Babylon, there we sat down and there we wept when we remembered Zion. On the willows there we hung up our harps. For there our captors asked us for songs, and our tormentors asked for mirth, saying 'Sing us one of the songs of Zion'. But how shall we sing the Lord's song in a strange land?

A Prayer

Lord, as you are well aware, I do not feel particularly well disposed to some people, especially those who push the boundaries of my Christian love, forgiveness and tolerance. As you are equally aware, that is not a hard thing to do. How shall we sing the Lord's song in a strange land? How indeed? Over to you, Lord. Amen

Do not worry

It seems to me that one of the most pointless things you could ever say is 'Do not worry'. Some people never worry and others are inveterate worriers, and whatever you say makes precious little difference. I notice though, that that did not stop Jesus from telling people not to worry. All they had to do was remember the birds of the air and remember that God actually feeds them.

Jesus was building here on the Psalms. Some of them – and you may find them irritating or unrealistic – seem to imagine a gentle world with rhythms and seasons and where nothing untoward happens. A song of thanksgiving is natural, and God is to be praised. Life is good: *The boundary lines for me have fallen in pleasant places* [Psalm 16: 6].

Maybe they were the songs of lucky people, or those who lived in a religious bubble which the harsher realities of life had somehow failed to penetrate. Or perhaps they were reminders that God is always with us, often in quiet, unobtrusive and gentle ways. I suspect the latter is the case and that these Psalms were there to be read when people felt overwhelmed with anxiety and worry. The antidote was to praise God, and that in itself tended to generate trust and hope.

If you want to read such Psalms try: 8, 15, 16, 24, 33, 104 or 145.

Therefore I tell you, do not worry about your life, what you will eat, or what you will drink, or about your body, what you will wear. Is not life more than food or clothing? Look at the birds of the air; they neither sow, nor reap, nor gather into barns, and yet your heavenly Father feeds them. Are you not of more value than they?

Matthew 6: 25–26

A Prayer

Lord, there are times when my anxieties get the better of me. But when I look at your heavens, the work of your fingers, the moon and the stars that you have established, when I wonder what human beings are that you are mindful of them, and mortals that you care for them, I become aware that I am seeing things from a new perspective. Thank you, Lord. Amen

It happens in the silence

One of Jesus' characteristic ways of speaking was to talk about the end-times. We find it strange and difficult language, but this was Jesus at the crucial and final chapter of his life speaking pastorally to encourage his disciples who will soon be at the very end of their tether. The end is fast approaching for him and for them – and it's not a comfortable feeling!

Again this is Jesus building on the experience of the Psalms. Many of the Psalms are complaints, or laments. They can express a profound sense of personal loss, or tragedy or humiliation (Psalm 22) or they can tell of something that has affected everyone in the community, such as losing their Temple or their freedom (Psalm 137). Usually they complain to God that things are not as they should be. Sometimes they complain that God is not listening; there is a note of resentment and self-righteousness. This is not whinging. It's done within a context of faith.

Then something extraordinary happens. They become aware that God is listening after all. It's as if something happens between one verse and the next, perhaps a note of silence, and in that silence something decisive happens. And things change. Such Psalms will often end in a note of praise. And what was thought to be the end of the world, tearing them apart, is in the end experienced as something more positive.

For such Psalms see, for example 13, 35, 86, 74, 137.

Jesus quotes the Psalms (22: 1) during the Crucifixion

When it was noon, darkness came over the whole land until three in the afternoon. At three o'clock Jesus cried out with a loud voice: 'Eloi, Eloi, lema sabachthani?', which means 'My God, my God, why have you forsaken me?'

A Prayer

Lord, thank God I can be myself when I say my prayers, that I know that you listen when I feel angry, disappointed or depressed. Sometimes it is at those moments when I think you are not listening that you are at your most attentive. Thank you for 'inclining your ear'. Amen

Singing a new song

Ever been tempted to play the prophet of doom? The country is going to the dogs . . . churches aren't the way they were . . . There is no hope for us . . . Then sing a Psalm:

Sing a new song to the Lord,
He to whom wonders belong!

Sometimes the Psalms sing a new note. Troubles have been overcome, difficulties have been resolved and a new and unexpected chapter has begun to unfold. The note is one of thanksgiving to God. What has happened is usually not the natural outcome you might have expected. Instead you get a sense of new life that God has brought about when it had just seemed impossible. This can happen to an individual (e.g. 30, 40) or to the whole community (e.g. 65, 66).

Many of these songs declare God to be King (e.g. 97, 98, 99). He has saved the people from their enemies and they now have found a new way forward and a sense of hope and expectation. What these songs declared about God in the Temple, Jesus lived out on the streets. He spoke of the kingdom of God, and the echoes of old songs would come flooding back. He healed people and gave them the faith and strength to live in a new way.

The Resurrection of Jesus is a song we need to sing, too, for that is the event par excellence where God has done the unexpected! And that is where our faith begins.

A Hymn of Charles Wesley

Finish then thy new creation,
Pure and spotless let us be;
Let us see thy great salvation,
Perfectly restored in thee:
Changed from glory into glory,
Till in heaven we take our place,
Till we cast our crowns before thee,
Lost in wonder, love and praise.

(*Singing the Faith* 503)

Time on our hands

One of my Christmas presents – a great delight – was Bill Bryson's book *At Home.* He wanders through his house, an old rectory in Norfolk built in 1851, room by room, looking at the history of ordinary things and how they came to be. It is a fascinating read and it struck me that this domestic format might prove a useful map on which to pen a Lenten journey in my letters.

Setting the scene, Bill Bryson points out that some country rectors in the 1850s weren't paid by the church. They lived off the fruit of rents and tithes and were very wealthy men. Some did the bare minimum of work and with so much time on their hands became experts in other fields. Country rectors used their homes for all sorts of sundry purposes. They were variously responsible for the first Icelandic dictionary, the invention of the power loom, and numerous novels as well as being pioneering experts in such diverse fields as dinosaurs, spiders, botany, telescopes and mathematics.

Jesus had had time on his hands, and he had used that time in ways no-one could have foreseen. He had spent the best part of three years at home with God. Ironically, that meant he didn't have a home of his own. He once remarked that foxes might have holes and birds their nests, but he did not have the same luxury. He had trained his disciples to be at home with God, too. And, now, as we mark the beginning of Lent this week, Jesus moves up a gear. With a sense of urgency he makes a decision that will have profound repercussions.

Jesus's momentous decision

When the days drew near for him to be taken up, he set his face to go to Jerusalem.

Luke 9: 51

A Prayer

Lord, couldn't you have just written a book or invented something? Or just stayed at home? Instead you had to go opening doors for other people. Me included. I know they were doors we couldn't have opened ourselves. I know you were about your Father's business. But I just marvel that you thought we were worth it. Amen

The view from the hall

You will probably have a hall in your house. It's probably a functional area rather than a place where you would spend a lot of time; where you hang your coats and hats, or from which you gain access to other rooms. But years ago the hall *was* the house. It was a large barnlike space with an open hearth where family and servants ate, dressed, and slept together. Separate rooms did not exist. Curiously the convention of calling the house the hall survived with large houses – Toad Hall, Little Moreton Hall.

This first Sunday in Lent is a time to celebrate. Jesus once took something that had perhaps diminished in importance, and he made it grand again. He picked up Israel's vocation to be the light of the world. *I am the Lord, I have called you in righteousness, I have taken you by the hand and kept you; I have given you as a covenant to the people, a light to the nations, to open the eyes that are blind . . .* [Isaiah 42: 6].

Open the front door of your house and the hall is the first place where light comes in. People followed Jesus because he enabled them – and he was not selective about who – to see themselves, one another, even their enemies, and especially God in a new way. Those stories of the blind receiving their sight were more powerful than we could possibly imagine. Now if your vocation to follow Christ has become somewhat functional, stand in your hall and open the door. Then listen to an old song: *The Lord is my light and salvation* [Psalm 27: 1].

Call and response

Arise, shine; for your light has come, and the glory of the Lord has risen upon you

Isaiah 60: 1

So they said again to the blind man, 'What do you say about him? It was your eyes he opened.'

John 9: 17

A Prayer

Lord, I have to say, I don't spend a lot of time in my hall. It's just a way of getting somewhere else. But today you stand in my hall and I want to spend time with you. I suppose my response to you has sometimes been functional. And you're going to tell me that picking up our vocation is a bit more than that? Thought so. Amen

Blowing a fuse

Somewhere in your home there will be a fusebox. At one time it might have been in the cellar, or in the cupboard under the stairs. Mine seems to have been transported to the garage now. You can almost forget about it. In fact we are so used to light and power on demand it's hard to credit just how recent a phenomenon that is. In the 1930s half of London's streets were still lit by gas.

Pre-electrified lighting was poor. Candles and oil are nowhere near as effective! And if it must have been hard to read, sew or much else in dark nights, there was one more thing. If people were driven to bed early it wasn't just the dark or boredom; they were exhausted from long hours of hard work.

And along comes Jesus who says extraordinary things: *Come to me all who labour and are heavy laden and I will give you rest.* Then he offered himself as light not just for his family, village, even his people. He offered himself as light for the world. Quite outrageous, really, when you come to think about it.

Jesus certainly made people see themselves, their situation, their enemies, their God quite differently. Hope does seem to energise people, doesn't it? And of course those who had previously seen themselves as *illuminati* were startled and saw Jesus in a quite different light, too. And that was when their fuses started blowing.

An invitation

Come to me, all you that are weary and are carrying heavy burdens, and I will give you rest. Take my yoke upon you, and learn from me; for I am gentle and humble in heart and you will find rest for your souls.

Matthew 11: 27

A Prayer

Lord, there are some things I can sort out by myself. I just press the switch and the light comes on, and then I get things done. But some of the most important things in my life I do best when I make a point of trying to learn from you. I just need a bit of help sometimes recognizing the difference. Don't give up on me yet. Amen

Pushing hospitality

Bill Bryson says that the first rector in his house changed the plans and removed the servants hall to give him space for a bigger dining-room that could accommodate up to 30 people round the table. Your dining-room, if you have one, will probably be somewhat smaller, but the tradition of hospitality – a very old one – is very much alive.

Jesus might have been forgiven for some of the things he said and did, but choosing the wrong people to eat with was a different matter. Holiness, for some, was a fragile thing and could easily be contaminated. There were unclean foods and there were unclean people, and Jesus was expected to avoid both. As to the first, Jesus pointed out that what was inside you as a person was what made you unclean. As for the 'sinners', he embraced them and loved them. Far from being contaminated, Jesus seems to have infected them with his grace! But this practice of Jesus around the dining-room table caused untold resentment in certain quarters.

Who you invite into your home is up to you – and Jesus prompted some searching questions even there – but our hospitality at church is something we offer in the name of Christ. If some people get ignored, now is the time to put that right. If some people don't know how to behave, get over it. The onus is on us to welcome and love them first. Other things will follow. Jesus pushed the boundaries when it came to hospitality. Follow me, he said. Maybe we need a bigger dining-room after all.

A frightening thought

Then Jesus said to his host: When you give a lunch or a dinner, do not invite your friends or your brothers or your relatives or your rich neighbours – for they will invite you back and you will get paid for what you did. When you give a feast, invite the poor, the lame, the crippled and the blind; and you will be blessed . . .

Luke 14: 12–14

A Prayer

Lord, no wonder you got yourself into trouble! Some people would say you had bad manners, speaking to your host like that! But I think I know what you were driving at. I want to thank you for those who have a real gift for hospitality in all its forms. I hope it rubs off – on me, first! Oh and thank you for that open invitation to your Table. I'm glad you pushed the boundaries after all. Amen

A cellar of grace

I have lived in a number of houses now, and some of the older ones have included a cellar. They have been dank, forbidding places, but because there has been no need to cover anything with plaster or wallpaper you get an insight into the foundations and the structure of your house, what it's made of and what holds it together.

The foundation for Jewish lives in Jesus' day was threefold – the Law, the Temple (and all that went on there) and the Land, all promised and guaranteed by God. If you questioned any of that you did so at your peril. Well that is what Jesus did – not by denying their significance, but by suggesting that the real foundation for their lives lay somewhere else: *I am the way, the truth and the life* may not always have gone down that well!

The straw that broke the camel's back was the cleansing of the Temple (which may incidentally have been in an underground area). Jesus believed that the real foundation of our lives is actually God, and with him the future is full of grace. The future could be seen as dank and forbidding, frightening but, no, it is full of grace. That belief meant that whatever the future held God would be with them and that gave Jesus the freedom to enjoy the present, love enemies, take risks and trust God.

Jesus' belief that the future was full of grace would be put to the ultimate test one Friday afternoon.

A parable

So then, anyone who hears these words of mine and obeys them is like a wise man who built his house on rock. The rain poured down, the rivers overflowed, and the wind blew hard against that house. But it did not fall because it was built on rock. But anyone who hears these words of mine and does not obey them is like a foolish man who built his house on sand. The rain poured down, the rivers overflowed, the wind blew hard against that house, and it fell. And what a terrible fall that was!

Matthew 8: 24–26

A Prayer

Lord, quite frankly, it wouldn't matter what I used to build a house with. It would fall down anyway. The wisest thing would be to leave it to someone else . . . All right, so you once asked fishermen to look after sheep! Not one of your wiser moments?! And you still want me to build? . . . Today I will start by thanking you for offering to be the foundation of my life. Pass us the cement-mixer. Amen

The plum room

The most enigmatic room in Bill Bryson's house is the Plum Room. It got its name from the colour the walls were painted, and according to the original plans was a drawing room (to which you withdrew, not got your painting set out). It then became a parlour room where only favoured guests were received. Later on it housed the rector's library.

I am not quite certain what the upper room Jesus used for the last supper was originally intended for. But that was where Jesus withdrew with his disciples to do what we often do, namely to celebrate an important occasion with a meal. This was not a birthday or anniversary but the Passover meal. It celebrated the gracious act of God when he gave his people their freedom from captivity long ago. In this place (where there was no library), Jesus spoke some words his disciples would never forget as they shared bread and wine: *This is my body given for you . . . This is my blood . . . poured out for you.*

They were celebrating, in advance, another gracious act of God. Jesus would be crucified. Plum crazy or what? But God's grace would have the last word. I suspect the disciples believed that God could act graciously in the past. But in the present? Under the curse of the cross? Can God really be with us in extremis? Then they felt the bread in their hands, and the taste of wine on their lips. *This is my body given for you . . . This is my blood . . . poured out for you.*

St John's version of the Supper

So Jesus arose from the table, took off his outer garment, and tied a towel round his waist. Then he poured some water into a basin and began to wash the disciples' feet and dry them with the towel round his waist . . . Peter declared, 'Never at any time will you wash my feet!'

John 13: 4, 5, 8

A Prayer

Lord, I'd like plum puddings, the plum appointment, the plum role. But you don't make it easy, do you? You won't let go of that belief that God will act graciously, will you? You take that to ridiculous lengths. And then you go with that simple towel and bowl, challenging me to live with that same kind of grace, too. It goes against the grain, you know. Lord, why are my feet wet? Amen

A most dangerous place

The most dangerous place in your home, unless of course you happen to live in a bungalow – is the stairs. That's where most accidents happen. In fact falls on stairs apparently constitute the second most common cause of accidental death – behind road accidents. If you do have a fall you will probably blame yourself for being careless, though if the lighting is poor, the handrails are missing, or the stairs are too steep you should be kinder to yourself!

Jesus died because he put himself in a highly dangerous place. He knew what he was doing. His parable of The Good Samaritan tells how an outsider crosses the boundaries of race and creed to 'bandage the wounds' of a man abandoned by those who passed on the other side of the road and who had been left for dead. He then carries the man into a Jewish village, where he might easily have been vilified and killed as the one who had committed the violence! The Samaritan takes incredible risks too, and promises to do more. And we are left guessing what will happen. Will the Samaritan get out alive? Maybe Jesus' parable is as much about himself and his ministry as anything else.

The religious authorities said to Jesus: don't go there! The disciples said as much, too. But sometimes you just need to go upstairs. And there was something in Jesus that made him confront his (outsider's) view of God with that of the priests and Levites . . . And also with mine.

The prelude to the parable of the Good Samaritan

A teacher of the Law came up and tried to trap Jesus. 'Teacher,' he asked, 'what must I do to receive eternal life?' Jesus answered him, 'What do the Scriptures say? How do you interpret them?' The man answered, '"Love the Lord your God with all your heart, with all your soul, with all your strength, and with all your mind"; and "Love your neighbour as you love yourself".' 'You are right,' Jesus replied; 'do this and you will live.'

John 10: 25–28

A Prayer

Hang on, Lord. You did all that – loved God and other people, I mean. But you didn't live. You died! And yet I still get this sense that you loved life and were living it to the full – perhaps like no-one else. Maybe that's the best way to live; maybe the best way to die, too. But if it's all the same to you, could we postpone the latter for a bit? Amen

The gardener

In the mid-1800s, the advent of the railways meant that more people could live in the suburbs and have more space. Suddenly gardening was to catch on and was no longer the domain of the super-rich. This coincided happily with the publication in 1841 of Jane Loudon's influential book: *Practical Instructions in Gardening for Ladies.* It gave bored, middle-class women permission to leave the rigidities of their domestic lives behind for a while and get their hands dirty.

One of the first people to experience the Easter gospel that Jesus was risen was Mary Magdalene. She was in the garden near the empty tomb and asked the gardener if he knew where Jesus' body had been taken. Practical Instruction No 1*: Don't assume the obvious explanation is always right!* The gardener turns out of course to be the risen Lord, and Mary's first instinct is to hold onto him and not let go. Practical Instruction No 2: *Don't assume life can possibly return to what it was before!* Jesus then tells Mary to tell the disciples what she has seen. Practical Instruction No 3: *Don't keep the good news of Easter to yourself.*

In a sense, of course, Jesus is the gardener. And as the risen Lord he may well have planted you where you are today for a purpose. Don't be surprised if you have to get your hands dirty.

Jesus appears to Mary Magdalene

Mary turned round and saw Jesus standing there; but she did not know that it was Jesus. 'Woman, why are you crying?' Jesus asked her. 'Who is it that you are looking for?' She thought he was the gardener, so she said to him, 'If you took him away, sir, tell me where you have put him and I will go and get him.'

Jesus said to her, 'Mary!'

John 20: 14–16

A Prayer

Lord, I know some people want to water down the Resurrection, but not today, Lord. It is the most fantastic, unexpected, uplifting news. He is risen! He is risen indeed! Alleluia! Words fail me. Amen

Expecting new life

You may be relieved to know that this is my last venture into the world of Bill Bryson's nineteenth-century Norfolk Rectory. This takes us into the Nursery. It is a modest-sized room and next door to the main bedroom. The intriguing thing, however, is that the Revd Masham who had the house built, was a bachelor. He was clearly a man with an eye to the future.

Easter is not the end of Lent, something that we can now put behind us with a sense of relief and get on with other things. It is the beginning of a new hope, the celebration of Christ alive and alongside us in a new way. Our worship (in the main) takes place on Sunday because that was the day of Resurrection and we are an Easter people.

And as Easter people we too will have an eye on the future. There is little to be gained in lamenting the days when there were lots of children in the Sunday School. Where there are children in our congregations, they are to be valued and nurtured – but not only them. We are about the business of praying for, finding and making new Christians, and then nurturing them in their faith.

The Revd Masham clearly expected new life to come to his house. There may not even have been a prospective Mrs Masham. But hope is a wonderful thing. Of course if you don't act upon it, it is little more than wishful thinking.

Jesus appears to his disciples

The eleven disciples went to the hill in Galilee where Jesus had told them to go. When they saw him they worshipped him, even though some of them doubted. Jesus drew near and said to them, 'I have been given all authority in heaven and on earth. Go, then, to all peoples everywhere, and make them my disciples: baptize them in the name of the Father, the Son and the Holy Spirit, and teach them to obey everything I have commanded you. And I will be with you always, to the end of the age.'

Matthew 28: 16–20

A Prayer

Lord, bless the font at our church. And help us to put it to good use. Amen

Strong words

Hypocrite! Now there is a word no-one likes to be called. It brings to mind someone who is pretending, or who is a phoney. It often grates because we have that nagging fear that it might just conceivably apply to us. After all, we talk a lot about love, and putting it into action, but if someone says we don't always deliver, who is prepared to stand up and quibble?

Hypocrite was a theatrical term. It meant an actor. Just four miles out of Nazareth lay Sepphoris, which was the capital of Galilee. The Romans built a 4,000–seater theatre there. It's possible that Jesus did some work there as a carpenter. Whether he did or he didn't, he certainly knew the term well and applied it to certain of the Pharisees with some passion.

Now don't get the Pharisees wrong. They were actually quite an impressive lot, and if they went a bit overboard on all the ritual washing and so forth it was only because they believed that all of our life belonged to God – the home as well as the Temple. I don't think Jesus objected to that. Far from it. *You, therefore, must be perfect, as your heavenly Father is perfect* was his uncompromising stance!

What Jesus objected to when he called people hypocrites was not their standing up for something that in a sense was beyond them. It was their self-righteousness he did not like. That might produce an oscar-winning performance, but even if no-one else could see through it, God could.

From one of Jesus' parables

The Pharisee stood up and prayed this prayer: 'I thank you, God, that I am not like the rest of mankind – greedy dishonest, adulterous – or, for that matter, like this tax-collector. I fast twice a week; I pay taxes on all that I get.' But the other kept his distance and would not even raise his eyes to heaven, but beat upon his breast saying 'God, have mercy on me, sinner that I am.'

Luke 18: 11–13

A Prayer

Lord, sometimes you used strong words to get your message across. And I accept that you have strong words to speak to me today, – yes, to me – words that make me wince and stand up sharp. And at the same time I rejoice that my fears and anxieties just melt in your forgiving love. Just keep chiselling away, Lord, I am listening. Amen

The 5,000 that listened

Today and for the next two weeks I want to write about the one miracle that appears in all four Gospels, namely the Feeding of the 5,000. Let's begin with the crowd. They came after Jesus, I suspect, because they had heard he could do remarkable things. He could heal people. He could make the blind see and the lame walk. They were probably little more than thrill-seekers who wanted to witness a show.

When Jesus steps off the boat they were an unruly mob, a rabble. Jesus called them sheep without a shepherd. In the next few hours they change. They become, for want of a better word, a congregation. They don't ask for miracles. They just listen to Jesus' teaching – for hours. They don't demand to be fed, but when they are told they will be they don't doubt it. When they are asked for food they hand over – admittedly, it's not very much – what they have got.

The crowd comes across in a better light than the disciples. The disciples are worried about other things – like getting people home, and worrying whether they have enough money to do what Jesus asks. They seem rather like the security staff who watch the crowds carefully at a political rally when an important leader is speaking but who are not actually listening to what s/he is saying. But this crowd does listen. They listen to Jesus, and they end up finding themselves part of something much bigger than they had previously imagined.

From Mark's Gospel

When Jesus came ashore and saw a large crowd his heart went out to them, because they were like sheep without a shepherd; and he began to teach them many things. It was already getting late and his disciples came to him and said, 'This is a remote place and it is already very late; send the people off to the farms and villages round about to buy themselves something to eat.'

Mark 6: 34–36

A Prayer

Lord, I think I would have reacted much the same as the disciples if I had been there. No, I know I would – because it is so easy to get distracted by things I think are important but maybe aren't, and which take my eye of the ball. Lord, today, help me to sit with the crowd, to listen to what you are saying today, and to receive. Amen

Loaves and fishes

Last week I wrote about the Feeding of the 5,000 and the crowds that attended. Today I want to focus on the loaves and the fishes.

Jesus has been trying to escape the attention of people. He had wanted to retreat for a while with his disciples. But the crowd comes after him, probably on impulse and with no thought as to what would happen later in the day. Jesus asks the disciples to feed them from their resources. They may have had some money, but certainly not enough. So Jesus asks them to find out what the crowd has brought. It adds up to five loaves and two fishes. The boy who has brought them hands them over to Jesus who gives a traditional prayer of thanks. And the crowd gets fed.

All our resources are precious. We may be tempted to complain we haven't got enough. At the end of the day – which, incidentally, was when the crowd were fed – the greatest resource we have is quite simply Jesus himself. But don't expect a magic wand. The 5,000 are not fed from thin air, but from the meagre resources of a child. Expect the risen Lord to use what you bring to him.

From Mark's Gospel

It was already getting late and his disciples came to him and said, 'This is a remote place and it is already very late; send the people off to the farms and villages round about to buy themselves something to eat'. 'Give them something to eat yourselves,' he answered. They replied, 'Are we to go and spend 200 denarii to provide them with food?' 'How many loaves have you?' he asked. 'Go and see.' They found out and told him, 'Five and two fish.'

Mark 6: 35–38

A young lad's prayer

Lord, there are disciples asking for food. I can't believe all this lot have come without any food. They are all shaking their heads, shrugging their shoulders. And now Jesus' disciples are looking at me. My hands reach out with my loaves and fishes. Suddenly they have gone. That's the last I shall see of them, I suppose . . . Lord, I could not have been more wrong. Amen

Food for a journey

The Feeding of the 5,000 leaves you wondering whether it could possibly be true. It seems to defy all logic and human experience. Maybe the generosity of the boy shamed the rest of the crowd into producing their lunch-boxes. Maybe it was just a story to get people to think of Jesus as a new Moses who also fed people in the wilderness. We would all like a rational, reasonable explanation.

But I happen to think there are parts of our faith you cannot explain. You just have to proclaim them. And when I read of this remarkable event what I want to proclaim is Jesus' staggering confidence in the generosity of God. What is provided is not 'just enough', not just a taster for a few people, or even everyone. The Gospels announce that they, all 5,000 of them, ate and were satisfied.

And what is left over fills 12 baskets. Now these were not rubbish bins, they were the containers travellers used when they wanted to take food with them on a journey. Presented with this almost ridiculously generous God, the crowd and the disciples are implicitly challenged by Jesus as to whether they are ready to take up their provisions and walk with him on the next stage on his journey.

From Mark's Gospel

Then taking the five loaves and the two fish, Jesus looked up to heaven, said the blessing, broke the loaves and gave them to the disciples to distribute. He also divided the two fish among them. They all ate and were satisfied; and twelve baskets were filled with what was left of the bread and the fish. Those who ate the loaves numbered five thousand men

Mark 6: 41–44

A Prayer

Lord, I don't know how to explain what you did, but I believe God is as generous as you say he is. And I am left looking at those twelve packs, inviting me to become part of a new people, ready and nourished for a journey of faith. I wasn't prepared for that, but a song is ringing in my ears: Feed me now and evermore, feed me now and evermore. Amen

Background checks

The Apprentice is back on the television again. Lord Sugar is once again in search of a promising employee and business partner. The potential candidates will be whittled down to three and then comes, for me, the most interesting part – the interviews. There is always somebody who has lied or misrepresented themselves in their CV or application form. And someone is going to do a background check and uncover it.

Background checks are important. Knowing who you are dealing with matters. You need to know sometimes whether someone has a criminal record, a poor credit rating, dodgy aspects to their character, or is economical with the truth. [CRB/DBS checks might be a pain, but they are undoubtedly necessary.]

One of the distinctive aspects of Jesus' ministry were his healings. Sometimes he healed people when they (or others) asked him to. He also did it a few times when nobody asked at all! Like the man by a pool (John 5) or the man born blind (John 9). Surprisingly Jesus does not run any background checks, a fact that would have really annoyed those who thought ill-health was something you must have deserved!

If Jesus asked people to 'Go and sin no more', it was afterwards. Jesus healed people and *then* challenged people as to how they were going to value the gifts they had been given. The risen Lord is still in search of promising apprentices. Our background and track record are not the decisive factors; it's our willingness to take up our bed and walk. More reflections on Jesus the healer will follow this month.

Jesus heals a man who has been ill for 38 years

'Sir, I have no-one here to put me in the pool when the water is stirred up; while I am trying to get in, somebody else gets there first.' Jesus said to him, 'Pick up your mat and walk.' Immediately the man got well; he picked up his mat and started walking.

John 5: 7–8

A Prayer

Lord, it's always someone else who gets there first. They win the lottery, get a helping hand, get the best seat. What about me? Well, I suppose, Lord, you knocked on *my* door, made yourself known to *me*, called *me*, died for *me*. I'd better be picking up my mate then. Amen

Breaking and entering

Breaking and entering usually does not go down too well. It must be very galling to find that strangers have damaged your home and possessions. At the very least you would feel a sense of violation and anger, not to mention fear and despair.

So how did Jesus react when it happened to him? You didn't think it had? Well, read Mark 2: 1–12 which tells what happened when four men let their paralysed friend down through the roof so that Jesus could heal him. Jesus had moved from Nazareth to Capernaum and in all probability this was his house.

There is not a lot of sympathy for this man. His family don't seem to be around helping him and he has to rely on his friends. If they were rich, respected figures the crowd might well have parted to let them through. But their access is barred. So, they break in and enter.

Jesus, far from being aggrieved and irritated, simply forgave the man. Actually simply isn't quite right because he spoke as if he were God doing the forgiving, which annoyed the living daylights out of some people. The man got healed almost as an afterthought.

The irony was as real then as it is today. It is Jesus who has broken into our lives with his gospel of grace and forgiveness – and not just for the 'deserving' few.

Jesus heals a paralysed man

He said to the paralysed man, 'I tell you, get up, pick up your mat and go home!' While they all watched, the man got up, picked up his mat and hurried away. They were all completely amazed and praised God saying, 'We have never seen anything like this!'

Mark 2: 10–12

A Prayer

Lord, pardon me, but what you call faith seems to me to be a bit of a cheek – and that's being charitable. Who's going to repair your roof? Lord, I get the distinct impression there's a big grin on your face. Forgiveness is no laughing matter. But apparently, you think it is. I'm working on it, Lord. Amen

It was more than a hand that was withered

The problem with familiar stories in the Bible is that they are . . . well, too familiar. You think you know them. Been there, done that, bought the T-shirt, that sort of thing. And then you are apt to miss things. It was a bit like that recently when I read the account of the healing of the man with a withered hand (Mark 3: 1–6).

For I suddenly saw something I had not seen before. This was Jesus getting angry. People were trying to catch him out, in particular by seeing if he would do something to infringe the commandment to keep the Sabbath day holy. The Sabbath was supposed to be a mark of freedom for everyone. Even animals and livestock were entitled to have the weekly breather from the demands of work. But what was supposed to be a gift had been changed into a weapon by the flag-waving Jewish nationalist lobby. Freedom had come to matter less than being seen as an observant Jew, or at least being observant for its own sake.

And Jesus was *deeply upset* at their hard-heartedness. He looked at them *angrily*. These are emotive words. It wasn't just the man's hand that had withered, others' sense of what God wanted them to do with their lives had withered too. Jesus dealt with the withered hand straight away. It makes you wonder if there are things we do as churches that get Jesus deeply upset and angry.

A healing that had profound consequences

Jesus said to the man, 'Stretch out your hand.' He stretched it out and it became well again. So the Pharisees left the synagogue and met at once with some members of Herod's party, and they made plans to kill Jesus.

Mark 3: 5–6

A Prayer

Lord, it isn't always easy to look in the mirror, but I hope you will make me aware of things I had not noticed before, especially those things within me that have made you deeply upset and angry. At the same I trust in your forgiveness, and your gifts of grace that can set me free. And having made me aware and free, help me move forward. Amen

High-definition stuff

One of the technological innovations of recent years that has now become fairly commonplace is high-definition television. If you switch channels quickly enough you can see the same programme on a standard resolution and then in high definition. The difference can be staggering.

When Jesus healed people it was often because he wanted them to see what he was doing in high definition. He once took a blind man out of the village to a quiet place and rubbed spittle in his eyes. At first he could see shapes; people looked like trees. Then Jesus touched him again and his eyesight became perfect.

Immediately afterwards Jesus took his disciples to Caesarea Philippi, which was miles away, on the coast. [See Mark 8: 22–30.] He asked them who people thought he was. They saw him, they said, as John the Baptist, Elijah or another of the prophets. What about them? How did they see Jesus? Peter told Jesus they saw him as the Messiah. It is a defining moment. They are looking at Jesus in high definition. And Jesus told them to keep quiet about it.

As Messiah Jesus would challenge the very culture and faith in which he had been brought up. It was dangerous stuff. It still is. We may settle for seeing Jesus in standard resolution. But once you have seen him in high definition, you will never be the same gain.

Jesus heals a blind man

Jesus laid his hands upon him, and asked, 'Can you see anything?' 'I can see people,' said the man, peering round, 'but they look like trees walking about.' Then Jesus put his hands on him once more. This time he looked hard, and his sight came back: he could see everything clearly. Jesus sent him back home.

Mark 8: 23–26

A Prayer

Lord, sometimes I have seen you as my friend, my saviour, my Lord. I believe you are that – but much more. You have come to bring your healing vision and energy to a broken world. Help me to see you more clearly, love you more dearly, follow you more nearly. Amen

Spending time with God

My letters this month will all be about prayer. Not that I have any pretensions to being an expert in the matter. Some people seem to pray with a wonderful fluency; it seems to flow effortlessly. Others make long lists of people they pray for. I have even known people who have kept prayer diaries. I have never been able to do anything like that.

I have also known people struggle with prayer – either because they feel they don't pray or can't pray. There seems at times to be nothing like the subject of prayer to induce an instant feeling of guilt or inadequacy.

I have come to understand prayer to a certain extent as listening, occasionally as talking, but mainly as just spending time with God. It's more than just those few 'spiritual minutes' when we make a slot for God in our busy compartmentalized day. 'Good, that's over; now I can get on with something else', we say with a sigh of relief.

Saying prayers is one thing; praying can be that but much, much more. It's an attitude of trust in God. Begin with something today you enjoy doing – whether it's reading, walking, gardening, pottering, working, watching television. If God is with us, he is with us. He does not have to be summoned. He is not going to come back later when you are finished. He isn't going. So enjoy what you are doing – with God.

From Psalm 23

The Lord is my Shepherd; I have everything I need. He lets me rest in fields of green grass and leads me to quiet pools of fresh water. He gives me new strength.

A Prayer

Lord, I thank you for those times when I can enjoy being in the company of others, looking in when they are doing their thing, and them looking in when I am doing mine. And for those breaks when we can have a chat. You know how it is, Lord. Amen

Blessed are you, O Lord

There are times when we will want and need to ask God for things. But the most important, perhaps even the most fundamental, act of prayer is praise. Now this can be confusing, because the idea of praising God sounds, well, rather sycophantic. Does God really need to be told how great and marvellous he is all the time? Hardly! He is not vainly preening himself in a mirror! Praising God has a different purpose.

A recent discovery for me has been the Jewish habit of blessing God. It involves saying a very short prayer, anything up to 100 times a day – not that I have ever managed anywhere near that number – for anything and everything: *Blessed are you O Lord who . . .* Do you remember *Fiddler on the Roof*? The rabbi is once asked: Is there a blessing for the Tsar? And at another time: Is there a blessing for a sewing machine? Well you can bless (praise) God for just about anything – from getting up, having food to eat, meeting people, getting you through difficult moments, having a laugh or even a good cup of tea.

It's a way of celebrating that God is with us in every aspect of our lives. Praising God is about seeing the world as it is, as a gift of God. And its purpose is to release the life of God in us – his gifts of compassion, love and hope.

Be joyful always, pray at all times, be thankful in all circumstances. This is what God wants from you in your life in union with Christ Jesus.

1 Thessalonians 5: 16–18

A Jewish Song [Quoted in David de Sola Pool, *Why I am a Jew*]

Lord of the universe I would sing you a song
Where can I find You, and where can I not find You?
Wherever I go there are You, wherever I stay there are You,
Only You, You, You, You.
If good comes, there are You,
And if, Heaven forfend, trouble comes,
There are You, You, You, You, You.
You are, You were, You will be, You, You, You.
In heaven and on earth there are You,
On high, below, there are You,
You, You, You, You, You.
Wherever I may go, there are You.

The persistence that pays off

Some things take time. We would like them to happen today or tomorrow but it doesn't work out like that. William Wilberforce had to submit to Parliament the same bill to end slavery year after year before it was finally passed. One American Senator spoke in the Senate every day for 19 years against genocide – 3,211 speeches later his bill was passed.

One of the things Jesus drummed into his disciples was that they should not give up. They should not give up on prayer and they should not give up on God. He once told them the Lord's Prayer (Luke 11) and then gave them a story about a man who had an unexpected guest one night. He had no bread to give him (which the guest would have used instead of a knife and fork to dip into the bowl).

The response of the man that he was asleep and did not want to be disturbed would have drawn hoots of laughter from Jesus' listeners. If anyone behaved like that the whole village would soon have known about it.

The man keeps knocking and eventually the door gets opened. Persistence pays off! Prayers are not always to be said quietly, gently. They are sometimes to be said passionately, forcefully, persistently. If you think God has nodded off then perhaps you need to speak up a bit.

And so I say to you: Ask and you will receive; seek, and you will find; knock, and the door will be opened to you. For everyone who asks will receive, and he who seeks will find, and the door will be opened to anyone who knocks.

Luke 11: 9–10

A Prayer

Lord, I keep praying for A. I am not certain it is making a lot of difference. In fact things are going from bad to worse. When are you going to do something about it? You must understand how much this matters. In fact, Lord, until now I did not know just how much. Amen

Getting the balance right

There is a side of Christian faith that is challenging and demanding. I remember Desmond Tutu once saying: 'God has a dream that we, God's children, will come to realise that we are indeed sisters and brothers, members of one family, the human family – that all belong . . . And God says: "I have no-one to help me realise my dream except you – will you help me?"' Or, as Jesus was apt to put things: Follow me . . . take up your cross . . . sell all you have . . .

There is another side of Christian faith that is less challenge and more help and comfort. Jesus acted out a profound ministry of healing and famously once said: 'Come to me all you who are heavy-laden and I will give you rest.' Now rest does not necessarily mean putting your feet up or getting shot of a lot of pain or trouble. Sometimes it's about finding space to get things right and get our priorities right.

Our faith offers neither unmitigated challenge, nor is it just the offer of comfort with no demands. A healthy prayer life reflects both sides of the coin. It's both where we answer God's call – I have no-one to help me realise my dream but you – and where we seek the grace of Christ in our lives. Are you getting the balance right?

Then Jesus called the crowds and the disciples to him. 'If anyone wants to come with me,' he told them, 'he must first forget self, carry his cross, and follow me.'

Mark 8: 34

Come to me, all of you who are tired from carrying heavy loads, and I will give you rest.

Matthew 11: 28

A Prayer

Lord, are you sure there is no-one else to help you realise your dream but me? There's hundreds of us! . . . You mean there's only me who exclusively goes everywhere I go? Well, Lord, I accept the challenge. Thank you for the grace and rest that goes with it. I am going to need a lot of that. Amen

Being honest with God

The Psalms contain some wonderful prayers. Psalm 108 begins:

I have complete confidence, O God!
I will sing and praise you!
Wake up my soul!

But then there are some howlers, too! Look at the next Psalm:

Choose some corrupt judge to try my enemy
and let one of his own enemies accuse him.
May he be tried and found guilty;
may even his prayer be considered a crime.

Psalm 109: 6–7

Psalm 109 then gets worse! He asks God to take away his enemy's job, then his life, and for his family to become beggars on the streets!

But what is happening, remember, is that this man is telling God straight just what he feels. He's not trying to be super-religious all the time. He is talking to God in a way, perhaps, that he would not dream of talking to anyone else. He is not trying to incite hatred. He is not trying to take justice into his own hands. He is trusting God – no-one else – with his anger, his fear and sense of betrayal. And maybe then, having been honest with God and got it off his chest, he can then go and behave quite differently towards his enemy!

Prayer is God's gift to us – not to make us religious, but so that we might get to know him.

Jesus said

When you pray do not use a lot of meaningless words like the pagans do, who think that their gods will hear them because their prayers are long. Do not be like them. Your Father already knows what you need before you ask him.

Matthew 6: 7–8

A Prayer

Lord, I am glad you know what I need, because I am not altogether certain I know. I am glad, too, that I can come before you just as I am, and not have to pretend to be what I am not. But Lord, I would like my actions to be directed by your strengths and grace, not by my fears and foibles. Amen

Hitherto hath the Lord helped us

Connoisseurs of different chapels may have noticed a particular quotation from the Bible that seems to have been inscribed or engraved in church walls all over the place. In tablets of stone, or painted above archways, there stand proud those famous words of 1 Samuel 7: 12: *Hitherto hath the Lord helped us.*

It's supposed to be a declaration of faith, but I must say it can sound exactly the opposite! It's almost as if things were set to go downhill as soon as the artist had painted his final letters on the wall. *The Lord has helped us this far, but that's your lot! You've had your rations. Now pack your bags and go home! Don't expect anything else from the Lord.*

Of course, it is not meant to be read that way! The sense is rather: the Lord has helped us so far. That's the kind of God he is; he will help us today and tomorrow, just as he has always done. So put your trust in him and stop messing about!

Well, do you really expect the Lord to help you? *Help*, of course, does not mean *do* everything for you. What God offers is a partnership, a relationship. The old Biblical word was *covenant.* A living church expects a lot from God. By the same token, God expects a lot from a living church. Or, so it has been hitherto.

Praise is due to you,
O God in Zion;
and to you shall vows be performed,
O you who answer prayer.

Psalm 65: 1–2

A Prayer

Lord, you know there are days when I don't want your help at all. I just want to get on and do things my way. And there are days when I just want you to get your act together and sort everything out without referring to me. Yes, I know that's not the way you do things, Lord, but that's not the point. All right then, maybe it is! Amen

Put in a good word for Jesus

A young Scottish Minister received some advice from his aunt the day before he delivered his first sermon in his first church:

> Ye maun mind, laddie, that they're no clever and learned like what ye are, but juist plain country fouk, ilka ane wi' his ain temptation, an' a' sair trachled wi' mony cares o' this world. They 'ill need a clear word tae comfort their herts and show them the way everlasting. Ye 'ill say what's richt, nae doot o' that, and a'body 'ill be pleased wi' ye, but, oh, laddie, be sure ye say a gude word for Jesus Christ.

It was good advice – and not just for Scottish Presbyterians! It remains as important as ever that we put in a good word for Jesus Christ. We find it easy in church to talk about the heating, the sound system, the preacher, the hymns. We enjoy catching up on the news of where we are all up to, mentally noting perhaps who we might pray for. We are generally less comfortable about putting in a good word for Jesus: *Jesus' words really struck home to me today . . . When Jesus spoke those words of forgiveness I felt he was speaking to me . . . How did Jesus find the courage to do that?* The sense of discomfort eases with practice!

Jesus said to the paralysed man – 'I say to you, stand up, take your mat and go to your home.' And he stood up, and immediately took the mat and went out before all of them; so that they were all amazed and glorified God, saying: 'We have never seen anything like this!'

Mark 2: 11–12

A Prayer

Lord, I hear your name a lot. It gets used by people who don't know you. And they make a travesty of your name. But when I hear your name spoken by those who love you I am reminded once again that you are my Lord, my Saviour. It's not just the things you said and did that continue to amaze. It's that you are risen and with me. Lord, help me to use your name with the respect, wonder and joy it deserves. Amen

And are we yet alive?

Occasionally in church you might notice the gentle cadence of deep breathing. The head is tilted slightly forward. The eyes are closed. The person in the next seat is pondering whether to leave them be, or nudge them, or check their pulse. Yes, someone has fallen asleep. I have sometimes wanted – but never yet had the courage – to announce at that point a change of hymn to: *And are we yet alive?*

Charles Wesley's hymn is always sung at the beginning of Methodist Conferences. It is a celebration of the ties that bind us in our faith and a moment to thank God for the experiences we have had since we last met. It is also a declaration that against all the odds we are alive!

And that is largely due to the grace of God. There is such a thing as a quality of life, of course, which takes us well beyond the fact of mere existence, and our worship, our mission, our priorities, our prayer need to reflect that. If one or two occasionally slumber during worship then I thank God that they feel comfortable enough to do so! But it is also possible for any congregation – large or small, 'progressive' or traditional – to fall asleep, too. We may all then need a nudge and our pulses checked. We all need to answer that question from time to time: And are we yet alive?

'And are we yet alive?' from STF 456 by Charles Wesley

What troubles have we seen
What conflicts have we passed,
Fightings without, and fears within,
Since we assembled last!
But out of all the Lord
Hath brought us by his love;
And still he doth his help afford,
And hides our life above.

A Prayer

Lord, there are times when I do not find it hard to fall asleep; it's waking up that is difficult. So Lord, I don't know what kind of tablets you can give me, but make me constantly alive to your word. I don't want to miss anything. Amen

A prodigal returns

Jesus was instrumental in changing people's lives – not for the sake of it, but because that was how you gave people hope. He never underestimated the cost – either for himself or other people.

In 2006 a South African film, *Tsotsi*, won the Oscar for the best foreign film. Tsotsi (meaning 'thug') is the nickname of a gang leader in Soweto. He makes a name for himself there through violence and a string of robberies. One day he steals a car, shoots a woman, leaving her paralyzed, and escapes only to realize there is a baby on the back seat. That proves to be a turning point in his life. He comes to love the child, realizes he must give the baby back and gradually we see him change. It's not just the baby he surrenders but also his image and identity. His puzzled gang members can no longer make out who he is – and really, neither can he either. He takes the risk of not knowing where he is going to end up.

That is part of our faith journey. We may not always know where we are going to end up either. Rather like the young man in the parable of the Prodigal Son, Tsotsi 'came to himself' and decided to take the risk of 'going home'. Maybe it's not easy to identify with a thug or a prodigal. But then there would be no point in God sending Jesus just to tell us to do what would seem blindingly obvious.

From the Parable of the Prodigal Son

[*The younger son*] *would gladly have filled himself with the pods that the pigs were eating; and no-one gave him anything. But when he came to himself, he said . . . 'I will get up and go to my father, and I will say to him: "Father, I have sinned against heaven and before you . . ."' But while he was still far off, his father saw him and was filled with compassion; he ran and put his arms around him.*

Luke 15: 16–20

A Prayer

Lord, it's blindingly obvious to me that you don't understand. I believe in you . . . you answer my prayers. Quid pro quo, done deal, covenant, however you want to put it! That's the way it works, isn't it? Why is it then, when I read about you, that I feel as if you have just left a baby in the back seat of my car? Amen

You have the keys

Jesus gave Peter the keys to the kingdom, which is probably just as well. If he had given them to me I would probably have lost them by now.

Well, I expect we are usually pretty flippant about that particular episode in the Gospels. We probably consign it to a mental file marked 'Catholics only', and think that its relevance to us is slight, at most. Well we could not be more wrong!

You might want to argue that the keys have been passed down a line of bishops (or Popes). I find the argument that the keys to the kingdom have in fact been passed to all of us rather more convincing. In fact, unless you realise that you are an important keyholder, you are missing something that is fundamental and critical.

We are about 'mission'. That's what Jesus has called us to do. He was recalling a time when if someone wanted the king's help, the servant's job was to use his key to open the door to the king's house and help him reach the king. Peter, and for that matter, you and I are Christ's servants. We can turn a key which opens a door to mission (through enthusiasm, care, encouragement and openness). Or we can effectively block mission by locking the door. 'We've tried that before. It didn't work.'

Jesus has given you the keys to the kingdom. You have not been left out. It's all a matter of whether you choose to use them, and how!

I will give you the keys of the kingdom of heaven, and whatever you bind on earth will be bound in heaven, and whatever you loose on earth will be loosed in heaven,

Matthew 16: 19

A Prayer

Lord, having the keys to the kingdom is a bit of a responsibility. Yes, it's an honour and a privilege and all that, but do you think I am up to it? Well I suppose you wouldn't have given them to me otherwise, would you? Now, where did I leave them? Amen

Itching ears

Do you have *itching ears*? It's not a complaint I have come across personally, though I understand it is often associated with the development of waterlogged skin in the ears and frequently occurs in swimmers. Though I am not sure that's quite what Paul had in mind when he wrote about it to Timothy. He was more concerned with people who were itching to hear what suited them.

He then urged Timothy to be sober (which I take to mean *clear-headed* rather than strictly tee-total), endure suffering (which is easier said than done), and to do the work of an evangelist (which he might not have considered his forte). I bet Timothy was itching to get a letter from someone else after that.

To concentrate on the third element, doing the work of an evangelist is not an optional extra for any of us. It is essential. Proclaiming our faith, presenting others with the challenges of the Christian Gospel have got to be amongst our top priorities. If we have 700 members in our Circuit we have 700 potential evangelists. It's not just a calling for specialists. It's something in which we all have a part to play.

It may be that your ears are itching and you would prefer to hear something else. But the truth is always the truth.

For the time will come when people will not put up with sound doctrine. Instead, to suit their own desires, they will gather around them a great number of teachers to say what their itching ears want to hear. They will turn their ears away from the truth and turn aside to myths. But you, keep your head in all situations, endure hardship, do the work of an evangelist, discharge all the duties of your ministry.

2 Timothy 5: 3–5

A Prayer

Lord, give us what it takes to quell itching ears. And give us an itch for proclaiming and sharing your Gospel. And make that an itch we have to scratch. Amen

Drinking from our own wells

Occasionally, some very kind people ask me if I am going to get these letters published. I haven't really given it a lot of thought. What holds me back is the suspicion that if I decided to publish, my reason for writing these letters would change. I started writing because I wanted to encourage the people I know, love and respect in their Christian journey. And that really hasn't changed.

One of the early Cistercian monks was a man called Bernard of Clairvaux. He once wrote: *In spiritual life, everyone has to drink from his or her own well.* He meant that you can't be a Christian by proxy, on the back of someone else's coat tails. You can't drink from someone else's well, only your own.

We have been going through a difficult patch. But the answers to our difficulties and the issues our congregations are dealing with will not be answered by people on the outside. Though, you may sometimes be tempted to think that the grass is always greener elsewhere. The answers will come from within our own wells.

My conviction that Christ calls us, and will use us, remains unbounded. We have to value and trust the particular Christian path that has nurtured us. Our wells may prove to be much deeper than we imagine, and well worth drinking from. And, as long as God gives me the strength to do so, and as long as people wish to keep reading them, I will continue to write my letters. Maybe one day . . .

The woman at the well, speaking to Jesus

'Sir,' the woman said, 'you have nothing to draw with and the well is deep. Where can you get this living water? Are you greater than our father Jacob, who gave us the well and drank from it himself, as did also his sons and his livestock?'

Jesus answered, 'Everyone who drinks this water will be thirsty again, but whoever drinks the water I give them will never thirst. Indeed, the water I give them will become in them a spring of water welling up to eternal life.'

John 4: 11–14

A Prayer

Lord, I am thirsty! I thank you for the wells you have provided for us. Help us to dig deep and draw out that thirst-quenching water you have told us about. Amen

Prayer and rejection

Perhaps one of the most difficult and painful experiences in life is to be rejected, whether it is by someone you love, by people you trusted or thought better of, or when you applied for something you had invested your hopes and dreams in. Rejection puts a dark cloud over the future (and indeed the present) and sometimes it can hang around for a long time.

One of the characteristic and defining aspects of Jesus' ministry was his love and care for those who were rejected – whether they were lepers, tax-collectors or other kind of outcast. He embraced them in a way that kicked against his culture and enabled them to look forward to the future.

Jesus died ultimately, not just a painful death, but one that expressed a total rejection of all that he had proclaimed and stood for. Jesus represented the best that humanity had to offer and the crowds and the authorities said no. Even if that meant cutting off their nose to spite their face. The resurrection declared that God refused to accept that rejection.

Many of you have lived faithfully and taught your children to follow Christ, only to see them reject a way you have loved and cherished. It hasn't stopped you loving them one iota. Keep praying for them – and also for others' children. Think carefully who you will pray for.

After the parable of the tenants in the vineyard

[Jesus said:] *Have you never read in the scriptures: the stone that the builders rejected has become the cornerstone: this was the Lord's doing and it is amazing in our eyes?*

Matthew 21: 33–41

A Prayer

Lord, can I confess my fear of rejection? It holds me back in so many ways. I am afraid of saying the wrong thing, maybe making things worse. I withdraw when a big part of me wants to go forward. I expect you were afraid of rejection too. Whatever it was that enabled you to overcome that fear, could you possibly let me have some of it? Amen

Breaking down a four letter word

I recently took part in a family wedding in an Anglican Church. The rural dean lamented that this church and others in the area had fallen out with each other big time – and this was not a good witness! I reassured him this was not just an Anglican phenomenon.

If we are living churches it is important to get our relationships with other Christians – and that sometimes means other Methodists – on a healthier footing.

There is a four letter word that gets used sometimes. It is *they*. It doesn't have to be, but when *they* is used with a sense of disparagement, dismissiveness or even contempt it can have a distasteful ring, especially when we direct it to our brothers and sisters in Christ.

Now *they* can be broken down into *the* and *y*. And the *y* in all this can be put down to things real or imagined, petty or not, that have happened recently or in the dim and distant past. It can be put down to fear, jealousy, stubbornness or just 'that's the way it is!'.

But *they* can also be re-shaped into *T* and *hey*. Pretty well all our churches have a gift for hospitality. If you should get invited to *T* make sure you find the grace to accept – and *hey*, you might get a taste for forgiveness, reconciliation, or whatever other gifts Christ wishes to send your way.

Paul wrote

Love is patient; love is kind; love is not envious or boastful or arrogant or rude. It does not insist on its own way; it is not irritable or resentful; it does not rejoice in wrongdoing, but rejoices in the truth. It believes all things, hopes all things, endures all things. Love never ends.

From 1 Corinthians 13: 4–8

A Prayer

Lord, I was just about to say, do you really expect us to invite them? They wouldn't come anyway. And shouldn't they be inviting us first? Then I heard you laughing, and I couldn't help but join in. Amen
PS: Thanks for the kettle.

The big brake

Methodism at its best is a movement. There have been a number of passionate forays into the subject of our being a discipleship movement under Christ. I would love to join them but even if I could write and speak in a way that was wholly persuasive and that could command universal acceptance amongst us all, there is one word I know that can make it all pointless. And that is the word *But.*

But it does not apply to me. But we are too old. But we are too small. But I am only interested in my church, not the kingdom. But we don't have the time, the will, the resources or the energy.

But is the big brake that can be so easily applied, a millstone that can bring any movement to a shuddering standstill. Sometimes *Buts* comes out too quickly. Sometimes we might accept something with our heads, then before it reaches our hearts the *But* has stonewalled the signal.

Some *Buts* are good. *But we believe in God. But we follow his Son. But we are given his Spirit. But Jesus was raised from the dead.* There may be other *Buts* that really need to be consigned to our prayers of confession. Time to take your foot off the brake.

Jesus speaks to a rich ruler who would like to follow him

There is still one thing lacking. Sell all that you own and distribute the money to the poor, and you will have treasure in heaven; then come, follow me. But when he heard this he became sad, for he was very rich.

Luke 18: 22–23

A Prayer

Lord, if I were the rich ruler I think I would have come out with a few *buts* of my own. Don't you think you were being a touch unreasonable? Or is it that you are asking me to follow you outside of my comfort zone? And that is where you are moving us? No *buts* then? Amen

Treading on toes

I would like to draw attention to your toes. We all have them; we're even familiar nowadays with the more technical term of metatarsals. And we all know that it is quite painful when someone treads on them.

One mark of a healthy movement, however, is that people in it don't mind too much having their toes trodden on. They tread lightly on their particular area of responsibility, and indeed welcome it when someone else offers advice or a helping hand, or even asks a pertinent question.

In a healthy movement we are not afraid we might be taking someone's seat, or of suggesting something new. We don't think that we are too small, or that our feelings don't count or what we have to say won't be taken seriously. We are not worried about putting ourselves forward for fear of treading on someone else's toes.

A movement has to move forward, but it also has to carry people along. More than than, it needs a vision that is not the province of a few, but one that is both shaped and shared by everyone. For that to happen, those in positions of leadership and responsibility need the grace to be flexible and do better than just smile through gritted teeth when someone treads on their toes. And those who are by nature cautious need to trust that, if they should tread on someone's toes, they will get a more gracious reaction than they might have feared.

Jesus speaks to his disciples

Who is the greatest in the kingdom of heaven? He called a child, whom he put among them and said, 'Truly I tell you, unless you change and become like little children, you will never enter the kingdom of heaven. Whoever becomes humble like this child is the greatest in the kingdom of heaven. Whoever welcomes one such child in my name welcomes me.'

Matthew 18: 1–5

A Prayer

Lord, I was just about to say that forgiveness, generosity of spirit and graciousness have a habit of going out of the window when someone treads on your toes – and what would you know about that? – then I remembered where the nails went. Amen

The nights the dogs barked

I have recently returned from a visit (with 16 others) to some children's homes run by a Catholic Foundation in Romania. It has been my third visit now, and each time I go something happens that causes an indelible impression in my mind.

It was difficult to sleep for the first couple of nights because my dreams were punctuated by the raucous sounds of dogs barking interminably in the distance. I suspected I was the victim of some infernal conspiracy. A day or so later came what turned out to be, for me, the stand-out episode of our trip. It was meeting a young girl aged 3 or 4. She was being looked after by a key worker in one of the children's homes; she was relaxed, happily eating a biscuit, and enjoying the attention of people about her.

But, just the day before, she had been found in the woods, with no clothes on and hungry. She cannot speak, can only bark and presumably her only companion for most of the day was the dog. Being loved is already having an effect on her. Maybe those dogs that I had found so annoying had been trying to tell me something.

There will be times when God is trying to tell us something, too. We may not always understand at first. Our focus may be too much on ourselves. But God can be as persistent as a dog in the night. And there is nothing quite like a child's eyes to remind us that if God wants to tell us something we had better listen.

Jesus heals Jairus' daughter

He went in and said to them, Why all this confusion? Why are you crying? The child is not dead – she is only sleeping! They laughed at him, so he put them all out, took the child's father and mother and his three disciples, and went into the room where the child was lying. He took her by the hand and said to her 'Talitha koum' which means, 'Little girl, I want you to get up'. She got up at once and started walking around. (She was 12 years old.) When this happened they were completely amazed. But Jesus gave them strict orders not to tell anyone, and he said, 'Give her something to eat.'

Mark 5: 39–43

A Prayer

Lord, you have a habit of breaking through confusion. You move through the howling crowds, to focus on just the few that matter right now, and then you tend to the girl, the one that needs you most. [I like the inconsequential detail that she is 12.] Then you leave a command to love in a simple practical way . . . Now you wouldn't be trying to tell me something, would you? Amen

A more excellent way

Some of the finest words ever about love appear in Paul's first letter to the Corinthians (Chapter 13). *Love is patient and kind. It is not jealous or conceited or proud . . . Love never gives up.* They are probably as familiar as any words we know in the Bible. But this is no celebration of love in the abstract. Paul is only interested in reminding the fledgling Christian community in Corinth that unless they get their act together and genuinely love one another they have missed the point. They may be highly gifted; they may walk the extra mile, and some may have the kind of faith others could never aspire to, but if they don't love . . .

Corinth had a burgeoning brass industry. There would have been dozens of tradesmen hammering away at the brass every day creating the most unholy racket. Paul wanted the Christians to understand that their words were just an unholy racket too if they weren't soaked in love. Surrounding Corinth were some hills to the north and the south. Climbing them took some energy, determination, persistence and time. It could be dangerous and on some paths you might want to turn back. Paul spoke of a 'more excellent way', a path that reached higher than all others. Such was the way of love.

In 1 Corinthians 13 Paul never mentions Jesus, but he was all too aware that Jesus had taken a particular path that was also very dangerous. He did not give up or turn back, and I suspect the way of love Jesus had taken lay behind every phrase, word and syllable that Paul uttered. Such love was not to be devalued.

Paul

Best of all, therefore, is the following [*higher*] *way. I may be able to speak the languages of men and even of angels, but if I have no love, my speech is no more than a noisy gong or a clanging bell* [*brass*]. *I may have the gift of inspired preaching; I may have all knowledge and understand all secrets; I may have all the faith needed to move mountains – but if I have no love I am nothing.*

1 Corinthians 12: 31–13: 2

A Prayer

Lord, you do realise that in Physics I rarely got more than a B–? I suspect I was rather better at Physics than I am at following you. I don't have any pretensions to being an A* Christian. But I do recognize, Lord, that your love is the real thing and if you can make some of it rub off on me then maybe the age of miracles is far from over. Amen

Dealing with cynicism

Love can be subverted. Footballers commit fouls in all kinds of ways. They may misjudge or mistime a tackle; they may get outwitted by an opponent and leave their legs in the wrong place. Sometimes their enthusiasm gets the better of them and they get over-physical. Nobody's perfect! Not even at Barcelona. But I have noticed that commentators have enjoyed employing the term *a cynical foul* far more frequently in the last few years. That's usually when a player blatantly and deliberately goes for the opponent rather than the ball, often with complete disregard for the spirit of the game.

Cynicism can enter any area of life and we should not think that we as Christians are in any way immune to its effects. Cynicism becomes evident when we don't expect much, or indeed anything at all, from 'them' (whoever 'they' may be), or ourselves, or indeed even God. Cynicism talks about faith, hope and love, may apply them copiously in certain situations, but then blatantly refuses to apply them at the key moment.

The answer to cynicism is not to cry 'Foul!' It is to pray for those who have hurt you, offended you, ignored you or rejected you. Cynicism subverts love but prayer takes us on the counter-offensive. Prayer is a way of loving people. It is actually very difficult to hate people you pray for. Of course, you may not change them, but God may change you.

A cynical question in the New Testament

Can anything good come from Nazareth? Nathaniel asked.

John 1: 46

Paul

Love is patient and kind; it is not jealous or conceited or proud; Love is not ill-mannered or selfish or irritable; Love does not keep a record of wrongs; Love is not happy with evil, but is happy with the truth; Love never gives up; and its faith, hope and patience never fail.

1 Corinthians 13: 4–7

A Prayer

Lord, thank you for confounding Nathaniel. He didn't expect much, did he? Well I suppose there's a bit of Nathaniel in me. Maybe I don't expect enough of myself, and others sometimes. Maybe I don't expect enough of you. Give me patience, Lord, and you continue with the confounding. Amen

When cynicism goes on a bank holiday

Last week I wrote about how cynicism can undermine and subvert our love. But it is not the only thing. There is also sentimentality. Oscar Wilde once said that sentimentality is what happens when cynicism goes on a bank holiday. It could be more dangerous.

Paul wrote about sentimentality in 1 Corinthians 13, not that he used the word. But it's what he meant. I have mentioned before the brass-making industry in Corinth. One of the things they made was mirrors, but they weren't made of glass; they were brass. A common (non-Christian) practice was to etch your brass mirror with outline figures of your favourite gods. When you woke up in the morning and looked in the mirror the first thing you saw was yourself numbered amongst the gods. Very uplifting, very sentimental. But Paul told the Christians 'We're not playing that game. One day we shall meet God face to face, and that is something to be reckoned with.'

Sentimentality happens when we fall in love with the beauty of the words. We may delight in all that Paul has to say about love, for example, be profoundly moved by them, but then do nothing about it. Sentimentality trivialises the gospel, draws our attention to those aspects that appeal to our senses rather than those that challenge or even offend them. Sentimentality takes us to Easter on the Good Friday by-pass. Sentimentality focuses on what we need rather than what others need and therefore the response of love gets muted.

Paul

What we see now is like a dim image in a mirror; then we shall see face to face. What I know now is only partial; then it will be complete – as complete as God's knowledge of me. Meanwhile these three remain: faith, hope and love; and the greatest of these is love.

1 Corinthians 13: 12–13

A Prayer

Lord, I think I might have struggled a bit with Paul. He always keeps you on your toes and 1 Corinthians is the easy bit! Lord, I think you would have been a lot more gentle and understanding. Apart from that bit about giving away our stuff to the poor, forgiving 70 times 7, taking up our cross, going out into the highways and byways, being perfect and loving our enemies. Hmm. Amen

The December dilemma

There's a particular issue that affects Jewish people in Advent and Christmas. It's called the December Dilemma. They can't easily ignore the Christmas lights, jingles and festivities; they may get invited to Christmas parties and they may even be closet carol singers! So what do they do when everyone else is celebrating Christmas? Do they ignore it? Do they treat it (like most people today) as a secular festival? Do they give a heightened emphasis to a Jewish festival like Hanukkah instead? How they approach the December Dilemma may have profound effects upon their identity as a people.

Well maybe they are not the only ones with a December Dilemma. We will certainly face the secular challenge of a Christ-less Christmas. That's what many people want to celebrate. It might not be our choice, but at least it's straightforward and by and large we have worked out what compromises we can make with that, and the ones we can't.

The real dilemma for us may be closer to home. It's about whether we choose to be Hymn 191 Christians or Hymn 193 Christians. *Away in a Manger*, for all its enduring popularity, is essentially a bit of religious escapism. Jesus does not even cry! *Born in the Night, Mary's Child* celebrates the birth of Jesus who comes to give the light of hope in the harsh realities of human experience. Whether we choose to be 191-ers or 193-ers may well affect our own sense of identity as Christians today.

Simeon's song

Sovereign Lord, as you have promised, you may now dismiss your servant in peace.
For my eyes have seen your salvation, which you have prepared in the sight of all nations:
a light for revelation to the Gentiles, and the glory of your people Israel.

Luke 2: 29–32

A Prayer

Lord, would it be alright if I sang *Away in a manger* just once? I know you cried, really. You were probably sick all over Mary and I expect you kept Joseph up half the night. I know people were desperate and frightened and you nearly got killed, even then. I know your earliest days were nothing short of precarious. Lord, I can tell the difference between glory and tinsel. Is it ok if I just hum the tune? Amen

Embracing the right time

Today I have been battling with the heating clock. This was once a relatively simply device with levers, dials and other components that you could see and touch. But the modern digital timer is a complex, fiddly, unforgiving and unfathomable little monster. You have to press *set* and *select* buttons in what appears to be a fairly random order. There probably is a logic behind it, but it has entirely passed me by. If the heat comes on at the right time tomorrow it will be nothing short of a miracle.

As you hear the familiar Christmas story unfold just look out for the time references: in the reign of king Herod . . . at the proper time . . . in the sixth month . . . in those days . . . when the time came for her to have a baby . . . today in the city of David.. You get the sense that this was a difficult time when Jesus was born – for everyone. But there is also the sense that this was the right time and that God got the timing right.

We don't always understand God's timing. The right time apparently is not always the most convenient or congenial time. One of the things to celebrate in Advent is that God is not deterred by the times we live in – then or now. He promises to be with us and the birth of Jesus is the most brilliant sign of that.

We may yearn for a simpler, less complex time, but this is the one we – and God – live in. Embrace it – as Jesus did – and we may well find that the heat is on.

This is the day

While they were there, the time came for the baby to be born, and she gave birth to her firstborn, a son. She wrapped him in cloths and placed him in a manger, because there was no guest room available for them.

Luke 2: 6–7

A Prayer

Lord, this day has had its frustrating moments, but I will ring the bells today. I will sing the songs that angels sang, because your presence today has left a taste for grace and glory. Amen

Sing your carols with gusto

The outlook, according to the news this morning, is gloomy. The country is heading into recession; we are going to be stuck for the odd aircraft carrier for a while and public sector workers are going on strike because of pensions. Not everyone, it seems, is prepared to take things lying down.

My own union has written to me saying I cannot go on strike because I don't get a government pension. But if I did have one it would be best to consider whether in my case it would be better to find different ways to protest! Going on strike might be detrimental to the interests of those we serve, especially the most vulnerable. It was an interesting email, if only because it recognizes that there might be a distinctive Christian dimension in all this.

Today most of our church services may well be Carol Services. The outlook here is decidedly different. The news is good; the bells of hope ring loud and the mood is joyous. Not that our carols ignore the world at large. The stories surrounding Jesus' birth include politics (King Herod), economics (gold, frankincense and myrrh), oppression (censuses) and poverty (shepherds). Our carols can be sung as a distinctive protest against those forces that diminish not only us, but particularly the most vulnerable – because God has given his Son in this unique way to set us free. He's not taking things lying down either. So sing your carols with gusto.

Mary's song

My soul glorifies the Lord and my spirit rejoices in God my Saviour,
for he has been mindful of the humble state of his servant.
From now on all generations will call me blessed . . .
He has brought down rulers from their thrones
but has lifted up the humble.

Luke 1: 46–48, 52

A Prayer

Father, today my songs are of joy and hope. *Hark! the herald angels sing* – and the forces that threaten to diminish us had better take note. I pray for those who are overwhelmed by the bleak mid-winter. May they also have cause to sing: *Glory to the new-born king!* Amen

A shifting hope

Sunday School prize-giving was always something to look forward to – for most children. The day when all your attendance stars were converted into a treasured present, usually a carefully chosen book. One year the children's names were called out in church. They received their novels and encyclopaedias and would soon be sent out from church to enjoy their surprise. What did I get (as the Minister's son)? *The Sunday School Hymn Book*. The scars are still with me.

From a child's point of view, I suspect, gold, frankincense and myrrh are equally naff presents. They would appear to say little about the wisdom of those who brought them! But then perhaps they weren't meant for Jesus – initially. There is a tradition in the Old Testament that Jerusalem would one day be honoured internationally. *Light will shine on the city and kings will come from all over and admire it* (Isaiah 60: 1–3). *Camel trains will come bringing gold and frankincense* (Isaiah 60: 5–6).

The only thing was, it never happened. Isaiah's vision for Jerusalem was never realized. And now the wise men go to Jerusalem bearing their gifts (to honour the city as a new king is born there?), but are diverted to Bethlehem. The light now shines from a star over Bethlehem; the glory of the Lord has shifted from the city to a child. Jesus would probably have preferred a rattle but gets gold, frankincense and myrrh. What we get is a transfer and shift of hopes from the city of Jerusalem to Jesus. At the beginning of the year, he is still the best place to invest our hopes. Arise, shine, for your light has come.

From STF 213 by Phillips Brooks

O little town of Bethlehem,
How still we see thee lie!
Above thy deep and dreamless sleep
The silent stars go by.
Yet in thy dark street shineth
The everlasting light:
The hopes and fears of all the years
Are met in thee tonight.

A Prayer

Lord, today's a new year. I would like to consign all my misplaced hopes to the past. Lord Jesus Christ, in you I place my hopes and dreams for the future. Amen

What did you say you were?

In my role as a prison chaplain people naturally want to know who you are. *Are you a Roman Catholic?* No. *Are you Church of England?* No. *What are you then?* I'm actually a Methodist. *What's one of them?*

Now not understanding what a Methodist is, is not confined to the prison population. Methodism today is not exactly what the business world would call a strong brand. Virgin, British Gas, Apple, Manchester United. M & S . . . Well, the next brand that comes into your head is not going to be Methodism. The problem isn't just that the world at large does not know what Methodism means; you would be hard pressed to find many in the Methodist Church who could give a clear answer!

You might say that it doesn't really matter. It's far better to put the emphasis on Christian faith and discipleship rather than Methodism. Besides which, a weak Methodist 'brand' might actually be a strength. We're easy-going, sensible, inoffensive and calm. People will like that.

Personally, I think it does matter. If someone asks us what it means to be a Christian of the Methodist variety what would we say? *We are just another group of Christians but not Anglican, Baptist or Roman Catholic?* After all, why should anyone join us if we don't know who we are and what we stand for? My next few letters will therefore focus on what some have called an elusive quest for a Methodist identity.

Jesus and his disciples went on to the villages around Caesarea Philippi. On the way he asked them, 'Who do people say I am?' They replied, 'Some say John the Baptist; others say Elijah; and still others, one of the prophets.' 'But what about you?' he asked. 'Who do you say I am?' Peter answered, 'You are the Messiah.'

Mark 8: 27–29

A Prayer

Lord, it's just as well Peter understood who you were or things might have hit the buffers rather quickly. Today, Lord, we have hit that critical moment when we need to know who and what we are. If you could lend us a helping hand that would be much appreciated. Amen

Something like the Bermuda Triangle?

Many years ago, when I was a Probationer Minister, I had to attend an interview, designed to test my knowledge and sense of vocation. The rather intimidating character firing the bullets asked me what I knew about the Epworth Quadrilateral. I replied truthfully that I hadn't got a clue. The other members of the panel clearly didn't know either and they raised their eyebrows at each other in the long, ensuing silence. Finally one of them asked my interrogator: Is it something like the Bermuda Triangle, but where a lot of Methodists have inexplicably gone missing?

Had we never heard of the Four Alls of Methodism?, came the disgruntled reply:

All need to be saved.
All may be saved.
All may know themselves saved.
All may be saved to the uttermost.

Indeed we had; we just didn't know that that was what was meant by the Epworth Quadrilateral. [Epworth, in Lincolnshire, was the childhood home of John Wesley.]

There is an inclusiveness about Methodism. We declare that the Gospel of Jesus is for everyone – regardless of age, temperament, race, background, gender or sexual orientation. But of course this has to be more than a bland 'Everyone welcome' note at the end of the notices. Jesus did not die for that. Our take on the Gospel of Jesus is that this is actually something we all need – more than any of us probably realise.

The four 'alls' of Jesus

Then Jesus came to them [the 11 disciples] and said, '<u>All</u> authority in heaven and on earth has been given to me. Therefore go and make disciples of <u>all</u> nations, baptizing them in the name of the Father and of the Son and of the Holy Spirit, and teaching them to obey <u>everything</u> I have commanded you. And surely I am with you <u>al</u>ways, to the very end of the age.'

Matthew 28: 18–20

A Prayer

Lord, you do realise that saying the Gospel is for everyone and meaning it may not be the same thing. If it's something we all need, and not just an optional extra for those that fancy it, then we might have to sharpen things up a bit, I suppose. Better start looking for those that have gone missing. How much is it to Bermuda? Amen

Living on the edge

One of my great friends over the past 20 years was a very small man. He suffered with polio, had an s-shaped spine, and walked with considerable difficulty. He confounded everyone's expectations: by going to school, then to university, getting married, having a family and holding down a job as a lawyer for 25 years. At his funeral we said he was a giant of a man – he must have been because we all looked up to him. Martyn frequently spoke about his life as living on the edge. The precarious nature of his health meant he could do no other. In spite of that, or maybe because of it, he was also a remarkable, wise, astute and very faithful Christian and friend.

What are Methodists? We are a small, vulnerable church, not quite in the shape we would like to be, if we are honest. We live, therefore, on the edge, not just of viability, but with the particular perspective we have gleaned from our pilgrimage with God. We have been gifted with more people than you might think who have experienced the grace of God in their lives and who have shown that in remarkable and special ways.

Living on the edge is how we describe any situation where we don't know whether we are going to sink or swim. We all find ourselves there from time to time. As Methodists we come together to worship God and learn from each other. And strangely enough the edge is so often the place where we find God teaching us (and testing us) to live with grace and faithfulness. Our calling may even be to live on the edge – because, well, that's where Jesus lived, I suppose. And he is well worth looking up to.

Jesus teaching people how to live with grace

If anyone slaps you on the right cheek, turn to them the other cheek also. And if anyone wants to sue you and take your shirt, hand over your coat as well. If anyone forces you to go one mile, go with them two miles. Give to the one who asks you, and do not turn away from the one who wants to borrow from you.

Matthew 5: 39–42

A Prayer

Lord, you met people on the edge: lepers on the edge of civilization, women at the end of their tether, men on the edge of violence, people on the edge of faith. You changed lives. Could I possibly have a bit more of your grace and faithfulness? Amen

Infectious laughter

Perhaps you will forgive a little excursion into history. In the early 1800s there was what amounted to a press campaign against Methodists. One columnist described them as *a perverse, insolent and factious set of wretches who have generally speaking been guilty of the most base and detestable crimes* (e.g. refusing to bear arms on a Sunday). A collection of articles appeared under the banner *An Attempt to Show the Folly and Danger of Methodism.* Methodist watchnight services and love-feasts were heralded as the occasion of eroticism. Methodists were 'melancholy and miserable', while their preachers were said to have unpleasant faces with features resembling those of Jews and Gypsies.

Well you can't always legislate for people's prejudices and misconceptions. Some would still believe today that Methodists are all tee-total, don't have raffles and only sing hymns that were written before 1875. What we have learned over the years is in fact to enjoy our faith, our worship, and develop a keen sense of humour. The sound of laughter rooted in a deeper joy is a common experience. [Yes, there are always some exceptions!]

At various times Methodism has been subjected to ridicule, near persecution, or has just been ignored, which is probably worse. The great thing has been to take the Gospel seriously without taking ourselves too seriously. [The opposite has, though, been known to occur!] The Gospel of Jesus presents us with incredible challenges, and the sound of laughter is often heard loudest amongst those who welcome them.

From Paul's Letters

Rejoice always, pray continually, give thanks in all circumstances; for this is God's will for you in Christ Jesus.

I Thessalonians 5: 16–18

A Prayer

Lord, I reckon the way to the Cross was interspersed with riotous occasions of laughter. Lord help us to enjoy our faith, one another, our worship – and you. And let it be infectious. It might even make us dangerous again, mightn't it? Amen

An evangelistic people

The first day I arrived to take up one new appointment as a Minister someone knocked on my door and said very earnestly: *I hear you are a born-again Christian.* Ah, I replied, that's very interesting. I believe I am, but I have a shrewd suspicion I am about to become rather a disappointment to you.

It's all too easy to pin a label on people. I have heard Methodists (whether churches or individuals) labelled in all kinds of ways over the years: traditional, catholic, liberal, evangelical, happy-clappy, dyed in the wool, bland, progressive, redundant. That's before the colourful language kicks in. But most labels tend to diminish people rather than build them up. At best they pigeon-hole and constrain them and at worst they demonize them. Methodists, at the end of the day, will prove to be a diverse lot of Christians, with different styles, emphases, and aspects of mission; and they will always be far more than any of the labels that get stuck on them.

Is there, though, a label that could be applied across the board? Well strangely enough, yes there is – and that is the term *evangelistic* (not to be confused with *evangelical*). However different we might all be – and that can apply just as much within congregations as between them – Methodists are an evangelistic people. We have a gospel to proclaim, to explore, to share, to live out. We might be evangelistic in different ways but we share the same message: Jesus is good news. It's a label that declares we are a movement with a mission rather than just another club.

From St Paul

For I am not ashamed of the gospel of Christ: for it is the power of God unto salvation to every one that believeth; to the Jew first, and also to the Greek.

Romans 1: 16

A Prayer

Lord, I want to thank you for those who are evangelistic in the ways that I am not. And I want to ask for your grace, so that the good news I share will be felt as good news by those who hear and receive it. And Lord, while we are on the subject, can you save me from the guilt of feeling I have never done enough one day and the self-righteousness that thinks I have cracked it the next? Amen

Ministry to one another

One of my earliest memories as a Methodist Minister was going to a meal at one of my churches. The hall was laid out for quite a large gathering, and people were bustling in and taking their seats for what was expected to be, and was, 'a good do'. I noticed that on the stage, four feet higher than all the others, and completely isolated, there was a small table with one chair behind it. What is that for? I asked naively. *That's the Minister's seat. That's where he eats.* Not any more, I said.

One of the problems of calling Ministers *Ministers* is that it's hard to think of anyone else as Ministers. But that is not actually the way we have seen things. [In official circles we get called Presbyters now. It may be a historic word, but I doubt whether it will ever have the same resonance.] We are *all* here to serve Christ, and that makes us *all* Ministers. People like me have certain roles and functions but it doesn't place us any higher than anyone else.

If there is a Methodist understanding of ministry it is that we minister to one another. When we pray for each other, share friendship, offer hospitality, visit, listen, do something on behalf of others, or so that someone else can be freed up, work with each other – and that is hardly an exhaustive list! – we minister to each other and often to a wider world.

Our separate ministries also take us into all kinds of different fields every day of the week. We may end up serving customers, family, friends, the community, particular people, whatever. But in, through and above all of that we are servants of Jesus Christ. Quite a ministry we share.

From an epistle

As good stewards of the varied gifts given you by God, let each use the gift he has received in service to others.

1 Peter 4: 10

A Prayer

Lord, thank you for the people you have called me to serve and who have ministered to me. Amen

Singing the Faith

A new Methodist hymn book has arrived: *Singing the Faith.* The first hymn book for Methodists was published in 1780 and 'the people called Methodists' have been singing ever since. We have also developed strong opinions about what kind of hymns and songs we like! A change in hymn book always brings a mixed response. Some good new hymns, some feeble ones; a sense of loss over the omission of much loved hymns; a bewilderment as to why some obvious contenders have been rejected. Then there are those who would probably like to ditch hymn books entirely in favour of worship songs.

Whatever your personal take on all that, I just wanted to say that alongside all the blessings that have accompanied the vast proliferation of hymn books, song books and projection systems that the years since 1780 have brought, we have run the risk of losing something that is at the heart of our identity. John Wesley's first hymn book was more than a collection of hymns. It gave people songs and prayers that would guide them on a spiritual pilgrimage from conversion to sanctification. There was even a selection of hymns for backsliders! The hymn book also lived in your home and was used daily.

We remain a people on a spiritual pilgrimage. Christ also calls us to encourage others to walk with us. The challenge now is to find ways that can sustain us on that journey. If we are not on a spiritual pilgrimage we shall end up slinging the faith.

Psalm 137: 4

How shall we sing the Lord's song in a strange land?

An old hymn in a new book [STF 444]

Day by day, dear Lord,
of thee three things I pray:
to see thee more clearly,
to love thee more dearly,
to follow thee more nearly,
day by day

Richard of Chester (*c.* 1197–1253)

Can you tell the story?

When someone offers to become a local preacher we ask: do you have a call to preach? There is a denomination in America – I can't remember which – that puts what is probably the same question in a slightly different way: *can you tell the story?*

We can all tell tales of dull services, but there is actually a strong tradition of preaching in our churches – Biblical preaching. Now *Biblical* does not mean we worship the Bible, nor that we take everything literally. We may not like it when people blaspheme, but we do not advocate stoning them to death for it (I Kings 21: 10)! Nor do we give equal weight to every book in the Bible.

What we do say is that the Bible tells the story of God's saving grace. It tells of people's struggles to get to know him; it tells of the decisive impact of the ministry, death and resurrection of Jesus; it tells how in Jesus people were brought face to face with the living God. It tells how God equipped people, sometimes the most unlikely of all, to become and live as Jesus' disciples. It's a story of failure and faith, grace and compassion, hope and renewal. It's about the passionate love of God for us.

Can you tell the story? Preaching is not just about reciting the Biblical events. It is about telling the story in such a way that it becomes your story and mine, too. It is about a living, unfolding story in which God invites us to become active participants. Biblical preaching takes many forms. It's at its best when it brings God's story and ours together and enables us to tell the story, too.

Jesus as the risen Lord appears to two followers at Emmaus

They said to one another: 'Were not our hearts on fire as he talked to us on the road and explained the scriptures to us?'

Luke 24: 32

A prayer for next Sunday

Lord, I want to pray for the preacher next Sunday. Be with her/him as s/he gets things ready during the week. It may be a struggle but give them the gifts they need to tell the story. Thank you for their faith, their experience of you. And make me and the others who will be there into the kind of congregation that brings out the best in them. Amen

Connexions

In many high streets now you will find an office called *Connexions*. They provide a range of services supporting young people and adults. Somebody, I presume, must have thought the way of spelling Connexions was novel.

In fact, the Methodist Church has been using *Connexion* for donkey's years. We are part of the Methodist Connexion. And the fact that we are connected is part of our identity. That involves loyalties and commitments (to Christ and other Christians) that support, yet supersede, local concerns. No Methodist Church exists in isolation. We are connected to others in the Circuit, the District and indeed across the country.

This 'connectedness' is part of our identity. Part of my first Sabbatical was spent in Aue, Leipzig and Berlin – visiting and preaching in the East German Methodist Church. At Mow Cop we recently had an enjoyable visit from a coachload of American Methodists. My daughter in Sydney has just booked a holiday in Fiji – where the Methodist Church has been subjected to considerable duress by the government, with severe restrictions on meetings. We look forward to a Minister from the Methodist Church in Kenya speaking at our Circuit World Church Service soon. We are part of a world church.

Of course being connected to people far away doesn't cost much. Valuing our connections with other Christians closer to home may indeed be more challenging.

Jesus said

My command is this: Love each other as I have loved you.

John 15: 12

A prayer

Lord, is that altogether reasonable? You have loved me with a passion, called me to follow you, awakened a sense of urgency about your Gospel. You forgave me, suffered for me, died for me, opened new doors for me. You intercede for me. Do you really expect me to love others as you have loved me? That much? . . . Hm. I had a feeling you would say that. Amen

Tagged as a meerkat

I was recently sent an email to say that I had been 'tagged' in a photograph on Facebook. So I logged on to see what particular photograph of me they had used. It turned out to be a very striking picture not of me, but of a Meerkat. When I moved the cursor over the Meerkat the delightful creature's name suddenly appeared – Philip Berry. [I probably need to speak to my daughter about this.]

After recovering from the element of surprise I looked at the Meerkat more closely. What struck me was his expression of complete alertness. Now I am no expert but I understand he was looking to see if danger was approaching, ready to signal others at the first sign of any threat.

Maybe Meerkats have something to teach us. An alertness to our own situation is important. God has given us eyes and ears. We may well be attuned to the 'noises' that threaten us. But Jesus wanted disciples who were alert in other ways, too: to their own weaknesses and motivations; to the needs of individuals and crowds about them; to the potential stumbling blocks they might find to discipleship; and to the call of God to discover and rediscover how their gifts could best be used to change people's lives. That kind of alertness is fundamental to mission. And Methodists without mission are only a club. [We probably need to speak to God about this.]

Maybe sometime I will see a photograph of me on Facebook, and when I move the cursor over my form the tag will appear: 'as alert as a meerkat.' Maybe.

Jesus speaks to some of John the Baptist's disciples

So he replied to the messengers, 'Go back and report to John what you have seen and heard: The blind receive sight, the lame walk, those who have leprosy are cured, the deaf hear, the dead are raised, and the good news is preached to the poor.'

Luke 7: 22

A prayer

Lord, where I am blind, open my eyes. Where I am deaf, remove the hands that block my ears. Make me alert, watchful, and ready to move not just at the sound of danger but at the moment when you call. And Lord, if I should fall asleep at the critical moment, send someone more alert than I to rouse me. Amen

Streams in the wasteland

Once there was a time when people went to church and there were no chairs or pews. People just stood in groups and clusters or sat on the floor just wherever they felt like it or where there was a space. Then in 1440, a gentleman called Johannes Gutenberg invented the printing press. The impact was felt everywhere – including churches. Before long everyone was sitting in rows, like lines on the pages of a book, listening to the authority figure [who could read and write] at the front.

Churches, if they have anything about them, evolve, adapt and change. Sometimes we need to rediscover things of the past. The core group in Methodist churches at one time was the class meeting or house group. That was where Christians grew and developed in their faith. Virtually all growing churches have house groups. That is an element in our identity in urgent need of restoration.

Then, sometimes we find new ways. People communicate differently today. I once asked my son who was ignoring me and texting away furiously on his phone: Don't you realise there is a world out there beyond the virtual one? Yes, Dad, came the reply, and I am talking to it! Finding effective ways to celebrate and communicate the Gospel today is critical.

From the Old Testament

Forget the former things; do not dwell on the past.
See, I am doing a new thing!
Now it springs up; do you not perceive it?
I am making a way in the wilderness and streams in the wasteland.

Isaiah 43: 18–19

A prayer

Lord, I am not always comfortable with the changes going on around us. But Lord, don't you let my irritation and frustration get in the way of letting people know how much you love them. You have given some pretty good gifts to help us share the Gospel. Help me to embrace them. And make them as effective as possible. May your kingdom come. Amen

Changing your routine on Good Friday

Mondays, it's washing; Tuesdays it's shopping . . . Sundays it's church. We all have our routines, and we like to stick to them. Good Friday comes on a bad day. We are not geared up for Friday services. That's when we usually do something different. You have to break your normal routine to celebrate Good Friday. You have to put yourself out. But then what happened that first Good Friday was no routine matter.

I intend to write about the Cross this month. That's where God put himself out. That is where Jesus put himself out – big time! We often deal with the cross by turning it into a symbol. It's a very powerful symbol, but remember it was also a degrading, violent and very excruciatingly painful reality. The Roman philosopher Seneca once wrote: *Can anyone be found who would prefer wasting away in pain dying limb by limb, or letting out his life drop by drop, rather than expiring once for all? Can any man be found willing to be fastened to the accursed tree, long sickly, already deformed, swelling with ugly wounds on shoulders and chest, and drawing the breath of life amid long drawn-out agony? He would have many excuses for dying even before mounting the cross* (Dialogue 3: 2.2).

Seneca was unusual. There weren't many people outside the Bible who wrote about crucifixion. It was too horrendous for that – no matter how widespread and routine the practice was for Roman soldiers. Why would anyone, why would Jesus, embark on a course that could lead to crucifixion? Why indeed? It might be worthwhile changing your routine and putting yourself out this Friday to try and find out the answer.

Palm Sunday according to Mark

People spread their cloaks on the road and others spread leafy branches that they had cut from the fields. And those who went before and those who followed were shouting, 'Hosanna! Blessed is he who comes in the name of the Lord! Blessed is the coming kingdom of our father David! Hosanna in the highest!' And he entered Jerusalem and went into the temple.

Mark 11: 9–11

A prayer

Lord, did you know what was in store when you entered Jerusalem? I know you had talked about suffering and dying, but did you really know just what on earth you were letting yourself in for. Did you really know just how hard it would be? In a way I hope you didn't. But I'm not totally convinced about that. That took some guts, Lord. Amen

A belter of an announcement

I thought at first I would spend a few weeks talking about the cross and its significance and then finish off my mini-series with a letter about the Resurrection. But of course that's not the way things happened. Easter Sunday did not come about after several weeks' reflection on the part of the disciples. It came just two days after the hideous crucifixion of the man they had loved and followed.

That's really quite significant. Yes, Jesus had talked about rising on the third day, but who among the disciples would have had the imagination and the wit to have grasped in advance the astonishing new chapter that the Resurrection unveils? What Jesus had said before would only really have made any real sense with the benefit of hindsight.

And on the third day . . . well what did happen? I don't really know, except that a number of Jesus' followers had some extraordinary experiences that led them to the inexplicable conclusion that Jesus had been raised. To say this was a remarkable intrusion of the unexpected is to understate the case.

Whatever God did at Easter could have happened Friday, Saturday or Sunday. It was just Sunday when people first got wind of it. The upshot of it was that they now started looking at this terrifying cross in a startling new light. What had been intended as an instrument of oppression had been turned by God into an instrument of hope and new life.

What Mary, Mary and Salome heard

Do not be alarmed; you are looking for Jesus of Nazareth who was crucified. He has been raised; he is not here.

Mark 16: 6

A prayer

Lord, is that it? Just a few words? I would have thought you would have taken out a full-page glossy advertisement in the national papers, but you announce the Resurrection with little more than a small ad in the local rag. Don't you appreciate how mind blowing this is? Mind you, it would make a belter of an announcement in the obituary column. Alleluia. Amen

When I survey the wondrous cross

When I survey the wondrous cross on which the prince of glory died . . . You know there is nothing wondrous at all about the cross until you view it in the light of the resurrection. It's just the sad tale of some misguided wannabe who gets slaughtered by religious and political forces too hot for him to handle. But the resurrection turns a different light on the cross.

Some years ago I found myself preaching about the cross in a prison. I had taken with me a small cross. On the back of it was a label which said 'a healing cross'. After the service as all the men were filing out one young man came to the front of the chapel, took the cross and clasped it with some considerable force to his head. He kept it there a few moments while he prayed a silent prayer. He had placed the cross precisely on the part of him that needed most healing.

The real cross was and is a place where people get healed, renewed and transformed. There was, rather perversely, something in Jesus that drew out the worst in some people – whether amongst the powers-that-be, the crowds and even his once enthusiastic disciples, and then having exposed that ugliness he meets that with extraordinary grace and forgiveness. There was something about him that not only stayed whole while he was being torn apart, it did something to others too. *Surely this man was the Son of God*, exclaimed one soldier at the scene. It changed them.

The cross is where you and I begin a personal journey of transformation.

A hymn by Isaac Watts (1674–1748)

When I survey the wondrous cross
On which the Prince of Glory, died
My richest gain I count but loss
And pour contempt on all my pride.

Were the whole realm of nature mine,
That were a present far too small
Love so amazing so loss divine,
Demands my soul, my life, my all.

A prayer

Lord, I stand at your cross today. I am told it's empty, but from where I stand today it looks full. I don't believe it's the end. I think it's a beginning. Do you think you could do something with me? Amen

More than a friendly caretaker

One of the first weddings I took taught me an important lesson. I arrived at the church to find the caretaker painting the front door a glossy red. He asked me what I was doing there on a Saturday. The penny dropped that I had forgotten to tell him about the wedding – and the organist and the steward. The church was still set up for badminton and the bride was arriving in 45 minutes. The caretaker tidied up, relaid the church, got changed and played the organ and nobody was any the wiser. He got me off the hook.

What would I have said to the couple? *I am sorry?* What would they have replied: *It doesn't matter!* I doubt it very much. In any case some things do matter, even when we say they don't. Jesus came, he said, that we should have life in all its fullness. There are of course an awful lot of things that can stop us having that kind of life. Some might be the very petty ungracious actions and attitudes to which we are all prone, and some are serious problems to be dealt with and horrific examples of injustice.

And to God, these things all matter. He doesn't say: never mind we'll forget about it and pretend it never happened. He says: I'll take everything you have that stands in the way of life in all its fullness; you can throw it at me, and I will defeat it. Then you can start living, forgiven, free and with a new power in your lives. But this wasn't a matter of sheer good fortune. It took more than a friendly caretaker. It took the cross and the resurrection to take care of that.

From Paul's Second Letter to the Corinthians

For Christ's love compels us, because we are convinced that one died for all, and therefore all died. And he died for all, that those who live should no longer live for themselves but for him who died for them and was raised again.

2 Cor: 5: 14–15

A prayer

Lord, I have never forgotten Paul. That's Paul of Bradford, not Paul of Tarsus. He was in the right place at the right time for me, and he knew exactly what to do. But then you know all about that sort of thing. You were there, in Jesus, when it mattered. On the cross. It's not just paint that's red, is it Lord? Amen

The sign at Heysham

Near Heysham Power Station on the Lancashire coast there is a stretch of beach. You can also see there a yellow warning sign: Unexploded bombs have occasionally been found on this beach. If you see what appears to be an explosive device, DO NOT touch it or pick it up. Well you wouldn't, would you?

Now the cross of Jesus does not look like an explosive device but it is. And it is important for all of us to recognize that. It's a place where people can come and be changed, where they can find forgiveness, and a new power station in their lives, and where they can find the grace of God. Make no mistake, God was in Christ on that cross, and he was there for a reason.

The cross was also a place where Jesus challenged and confronted the very forces that controlled and damaged people's lives. He took on some pretty heavy political and religious authorities. They thought the cross would be a convenient public statement that you should not mess with them. Two days after the crucifixion it had become a public statement that God had played his trump card.

You may occasionally see a cross as you walk about. It's more explosive than you might think. Don't hesitate to pick it up.

Remember what Jesus had said earlier

Then he said to them all: 'Whoever wants to be my disciple must deny themselves and take up their cross daily and follow me.'

Luke 9: 23

A prayer

Lord, forgive me when I have taken your cross lightly, when I have just regarded it as a symbol to be polished and admired from a distance. Forgive me when I have been ashamed of it. Today as I take it up again help me to understand how powerful it was in certain hands, and how explosive it was in yours. Change me by your grace, and give me the grace to challenge the very things Jesus did. I take up this cross, and I follow you. Amen

The secrets of our hearts

The Wind in the Willows has delighted both children and adults for years. Kenneth Grahame's book about Ratty, Mole, Badger and the infamous Mr Toad was the subject of a recent television documentary presented by Griff Rhys Jones. It celebrated not only the delights of 'messing about in boats' but let you into one or two secrets. Grahame wrote the book primarily for his son who was socially rather gauche and who indeed had something of the unloveable but much loved Mr Toad about him.

Jesus found his earliest disciples messing about in boats – not by the riverside, but by the Sea of Galilee. That lake, too, held its secrets. In January 1986, the water levels of the lake had dropped because of droughts and a remarkable discovery was found on the lake bed – a fishing boat from the time of Jesus. And that might be the least significant of the Sea of Galilee's secrets.

Why did those first fishermen follow Jesus? Because he touched some of their secret hopes, dreams or aspirations? All of us have secrets – no matter which way the wind has blown in our willows. That applies even when we are more like Ratty, Mole and Badger than Mr Toad. We may have secret regrets, dreams, longings or histories. They may be just below the surface or deeply submerged. The one person we can always open them up to remains Jesus. Don't be surprised then if God starts sharing some of his secrets with you. As one lady once said: I knew God loved me, but I never knew just how much.

From the Old Testament

Call to me and I will answer you and tell you wonderful and marvellous things that you know nothing about.

Jeremiah 33: 3

A prayer

Lord, you know the secrets of all our hearts, even the things we keep hidden from ourselves. It is good to know that we can come to you and tell you whatever we like without being afraid. And, Lord, I come with a mixture of anticipation and apprehension – for what secrets have you laid upon your heart to tell us? Amen

The Sea of Galilee

This month I am focussing on the Sea of Galilee. Jesus seems to have made Capernaum, a fishing village on the shore, his home. Fish and fishermen, boats and nets figure large in the gospels' stories. He told parables about nets, fed the 5,000 with loaves and fishes, calmed the storm and helped his disciples make some remarkable catches.

It makes you wonder why Jesus, whose background was in carpentry not the fishing industry, headed for the Sea of Galilee in search of suitable disciples. Well Galilee had changed in the past 10 years. A new city had sprung up on the shores called Tiberias. It was part of King Herod's (Antipas) plan to curry favour with the Roman Emperor – whose name, not surprisingly, was Tiberias. The impact on the local fishing industry in other villages would have been devastating with new regulations and taxes by the score. Soon they would have no fish to sell.

In some quarters, the lake became known as the Sea of Tiberias. When Jesus asked those fishermen to follow him, maybe they felt that this would be the start of something that would in the end enable them to reclaim their livelihoods. Jesus might be able to reclaim the Sea from Tiberias for God. And in a way he was doing that – but probably on a much bigger compass than any of the disciples would have guessed at the time.

Jesus appears to his disciples after the resurrection

Simon Peter, Thomas (also known as Didymus), Nathanael from Cana in Galilee, the sons of Zebedee, and two other disciples were together. 'I'm going out to fish,' Simon Peter told them, and they said, 'We'll go with you.' So they went out and got into the boat, but that night they caught nothing. Early in the morning, Jesus stood on the shore, but the disciples did not realize that it was Jesus. He called out to them, 'Friends, haven't you any fish?' 'No,' they answered.

John 21: 2–5

A prayer

Lord, I expect you went to the Lake for a bit more than relaxation and a tranquil view. The world has changed a lot for us in the past 10 years, and I am glad I can trust you to be around at the critical moment, like you were then. I wonder, too, what you would like to reclaim for your kingdom today. Amen

A poor sailor

I would never have made a great sailor. My first crossing of the Channel took six hours in the face of gale force winds. It was not a pleasant experience, for it wasn't just the sea that was heaving. One of the most famous incidents in the gospels is of Jesus stilling the storm on the Sea of Galilee. Had I been there, I would not have said a word of complaint to Jesus, like the disciples did. I would have long since lost the will to live.

The Sea of Galilee can be serenely beautiful, but sharp winds can whip it up into quite a frenzy. I wonder whether any of the disciples might just for a moment have considered throwing Jesus overboard. Those who remember the story of Jonah will recognize a Biblical precedent. But if they harboured any such thoughts they kept them to themselves. They simply asked Jesus if he would care to wake up and consider their fairly dire predicament.

Jesus then stills the storm, and asks them whey they were so frightened. Had they no faith? That connection between fear and faith is an interesting one. The opposite of faith is not doubt. It's fear. It would be fear that would prevent those disciples following Jesus all the way to the Cross when another storm was reaching its height. We all have fears from time to time. Sometimes we find ourselves in the wrong boat. Faith does not remove fears, but it can stop them overwhelming us.

Jesus picks up on an Old Testament theme

Do not fear, for I have redeemed you; I have summoned you by name; you are mine.

When you pass through the waters, I will be with you; and when you pass through the rivers, they will not sweep over you. When you walk through the fire, you will not be burned; the flames will not set you ablaze. For I am the LORD your God, the Holy One of Israel, your Saviour . . . you are precious and honoured in my sight . . . Do not be afraid, for I am with you.

From Isaiah 43: 2–5

A prayer

Lord, when we are afraid to face or tell the truth, be with us. When we are afraid we have nothing left to give or we are at our wits end, we count on you to sustain us. When we are afraid for others give us the grace to give them what they truly need. And when our fears are ruling our hearts and lives threatening to overwhelm us, we ask that we too will then find the wisdom and strength to ask for your faith and calm. Amen

The postscript

P.S. Don't forget to put the cat out. You know what it is like when you get a letter. It's all finished. It's all been signed and then someone has remembered something very important. So you get a P.S. And you ignore it, at your peril, because you can bet your life some highly significant instruction has been given to you and you are now expected to take responsibility for it.

John ends his Gospel at chapter 20. It's followed by a P.S. namely, chapter 21. In short it runs: P.S. Don't forget the stranger on the shore.

What stranger on the shore? Peter goes back to Galilee. The excitement of the Resurrection is over and now what? He decides to pick up the pieces of his old life again and go back to his job as a fisherman. He wasn't doing too well until the stranger on the shore yells across some friendly if somewhat nonsensical advice: put your nets out on the other side of the boat. As if that's going to make any difference. But, as luck would have it the nets were soon full to bursting.

Peter did not recognize the risen Lord at first. It's only now – in the postscript – that he recognizes fully who Jesus is. It's his *This is my beloved son in whom I am well pleased* moment. With that Peter the fisherman is commissioned by Jesus as a pastor: *Feed my sheep.*

P.S. The Resurrection is not the end. It's a new beginning. When you have put the cat out, you will still have new responsibilities.

Meeting the stranger on the shore

The other disciples followed [*Peter*]*in the boat, towing the net full of fish, for they were not far from shore, about a hundred yards. When they landed, they saw a fire of burning coals there with fish on it, and some bread. Jesus said to them, 'Bring some of the fish you have just caught.' So Simon Peter climbed back into the boat and dragged the net ashore. It was full of large fish, 153, but even with so many the net was not torn. Jesus said to them, 'Come and have breakfast.'*

John 21: 8–12

A prayer

Lord, I can't get my head around the fish. Who was the anorak who counted that lot? But there is something inherently powerful in that picture of you cooking an expected barbecue breakfast for your disciples. Is there anything left, Lord? Amen

Seeing things differently

I heard recently of a scenario that was given to people being interviewed for a job: You are driving along in your car on a wild, stormy night. You pass by a bus stop, and you see three people waiting for the bus:

1. An old lady who looks as if she is about to die.
2. An old friend who once saved your life.
3. The perfect man (or) woman you have been dreaming about.

The interviewees were then asked which one would they choose to offer a ride to, knowing that there could only be one passenger in your car.

Some picked the old lady, because she was going to die – she needed to be saved first; others picked the old friend because this would be the perfect chance to pay him back. Others reckoned they might never be able to find their dream lover again. So they picked her.

The man who got the job said: 'I would give the car keys to my old friend, and let him take the lady to the hospital, then I would stay behind and wait for the bus with the woman of my dreams.'

He saw things differently. One of the gifts of the Holy Spirit is to enable us to see things differently. That means seeing other people differently, seeing ourselves differently, seeing our churches differently. I allowed myself a little chuckle at that scenario above. What God's Spirit allows us is to laugh at impossibilities and see new ways forward. Not because we are clever, but because his Spirit is at work.

Jesus and blind Bartimaeus

Many rebuked [Bartimaeus] and told him to be quiet, but he shouted all the more, 'Son of David, have mercy on me!' Jesus stopped and said, 'Call him.' So they called to the blind man, 'Cheer up! On your feet! He's calling you.' Throwing his cloak aside, he jumped to his feet and came to Jesus. 'What do you want me to do for you?' Jesus asked him. The blind man said, 'Rabbi, I want to see.' 'Go,' said Jesus, 'your faith has healed you.' Immediately he received his sight and followed Jesus along the road.

Mark 10: 48–52

A prayer

Lord, now don't you stop with Bartimaeus. You can open his eyes, so you can open mine. Give me your Spirit that enables me to see, and not only to see but to see things differently – the way you see them. Amen

The Comforter

What do you think of when someone says the word 'comfort' to you. A whole host of images may come to mind – the security blanket you had as a child, the support of friends or family in difficult times, a level of financial security or little in the way to worry about, or just something you stick in the washing machine to make your clothes softer.

One of the ways in which Jesus spoke of the Holy Spirit was as the Comforter, only this might not be quite as it sounds to modern ears. This is not God just being sympathetic to you in trying circumstances. The Comforter is the one who brings Good News from God, and who confirms it with signs. Jesus 'comforted' those who had been ignored or who had lost hope. He gave them forgiveness, and a new sense of being valued and called them to something new.

He promised the Holy Spirit as the Comforter. It was a great 'comfort' to the early church when Peter converted a Roman soldier (Acts 10) and this first pagan (Cornelius) was baptized and entered the church. It was the Spirit who comforted Peter with the knowledge that there was no distinction between the faith of a Jewish Christian and a Gentile Christian. But of course while this might have been good news for some (comforting) it was profoundly disturbing to others!

What is the Comforter up to in your neck of the woods?

The Comforter at work

And so it was that the church throughout Judea, Galilee and Samaria had a time of peace. Through the help of the Holy Spirit it was strengthened and grew in numbers, as it lived in reverence for the Lord.

Acts 9: 31

A prayer

Lord, well that's all very well. Lovely to have a church where everyone gets on well together all the time, when new people keep rolling in, the building maintains itself and when no-one is asking you for a bit more in the collection . . . And yet I remember the Spirit sustained you and Peter and John when there were tougher times and when you suffered for us . . . so, Lord, I have slowly come to the conclusion that we can trust your Spirit to give us good news in all weathers. Give us the eyes to see where that's happening, and the heart to welcome Him. Amen

The prompt

Spellcheckers don't get everything. Your mis-spelling turns out to be a real word, so the spellchecker doesn't notice. But it can also be you that doesn't notice. When you write something the worst thing you can do is to check it yourself. Ask any proof-reader. We are not always looking for the right things, so certain things escape our attention.

Jesus called the Holy Spirit the Spirit of Truth. I take that as a way of saying: God notices the things you don't. You might be so used to doing things in a certain way, you might not be noticing when God is asking you to do things in a different way. You might be so wedded to your principles that you don't notice that life and spontaneity have gone out of the window. You may be so taken by what you believe is right that you didn't notice you forgot the basics – to love, as Jesus loved.

When the Holy Spirit is alive in us, he asks questions. They might be about our presumptions, our priorities, our certainties. What are you looking for? Where is your brother? What are you doing here? The Spirit of Truth is just God doing nothing more (and nothing less) than prompting us to live by the truth we have found in Jesus. He notices the things we don't, the people we have missed, the wrong turning we took. He's kind of polishing our glasses so we can see more clearly, and proof-reading our lives so we don't make the assumption we have got it all sussed. He's worth paying attention to.

The Work of the Holy Spirit

When the Spirit comes, who reveals the truth about God, he will lead you into all the truth

John 16: 13

A prayer

Lord, it's not always easy to focus on the right things all of the time. Sometimes I understand one thing as clearly as anything and then totally miss the point in something else. Lord, you promise to come to us as the Spirit of Truth. Just help me notice where you are pointing, and keep asking the questions when I don't get it. Amen

The yellow plastic hat

My neighbours have been building an extension. It's an exciting time. Plans that may have been on the drawing board for a long time are being put into effect. What's being built is hidden from view; it's all going on round the back. But you can tell something is happening. Lorry loads of steel, bricks and sand appear; contractors' vans fill the drive. The tell-tale sounds of hammers clanging and saws humming tell you that big changes are taking place.

Building something can be a busy time, too. There's a lot to be done. Bricklayers, carpenters, electricians, plumbers and plasterers, all have to be fitted in – and at the right time. It can also be a frustrating time. There's a lot of noise and dust. You are forever cleaning and dusting. [Well, maybe not all of us!] The unforeseen happens and delays are inevitable. Something arrives broken and getting it replaced might not be that easy. Maybe one of the key contractors decides to go on holiday for a week or two.

But at the end of the day, it's a fulfilling time. My neighbours will be able to look at their house. So too will the contractors and the architects, the contractors, the painters and decorators. They'll be able to say: *We built that. We had hold-ups and difficulties; we had all sorts of obstacles to overcome. It was hard work, but we built it – together.*

Now Jesus is still about the business of building his church. [And he wasn't talking buildings.] He calls us to extend his mission and ministry. St Paul used to say women ought to come to church with a hat on. Actually we should all be coming to church with a hat on. A yellow plastic one will do nicely. Because it's good to be properly dressed.

Jesus makes his intentions clear

And I tell you, you are Peter, and on this rock I will build my church, and the gates of hell shall not prevail against it.

Matthew 16: 18

A prayer

Lord, I expect Peter must have been pretty excited and perhaps a bit perplexed when you told him you were going to build your church on him. I suppose you mean you're going to extend it too around the likes of us. Lord, we do 'perplexed' quite well. It's probably more in the area of 'excitement' that we need a little help. Amen

Giving others a sense of ownership

One of my favourite writers is Jonathan Sacks, the Chief Rabbi. One of his books is called *The Home We Build Together.* It's really about culture and society, but there are some interesting perspectives we can draw from it when thinking about the church we build together.

Sacks tells the parable of 100 people scouring the countryside for a place to stay. They come to the owner of a large country house and he gives them a warm smile. *How good to see you,* he says. *As you can see I have an enormous home. Far too big for me. There are 100s of empty rooms. Stay as long as you like. I look forward to your company. From now on consider yourself my guests.*

It sounds good. It's welcoming and the hospitality is certainly not in short supply. But it is never going to be their home. They will stay for a while, but really, it belongs to someone else. They will never be able to change anything in the country house because they will never have a real say. If we want to see Jesus build his church in us, we have to give people a sense of ownership. Otherwise it will always be 'your church' and not 'ours'.

Building a church isn't just about filling the empty rooms or, as we would say, putting bums on seats – though remember, it isn't not about that either! It's about encouraging people to see that they can play a real part in what Christ is building today. And the owners of the large country houses may not always find that quite so easy.

Jesus shares his authority

I will give you [Peter] the keys of the kingdom of heaven; whatever you bind on earth will be bound in heaven, and whatever you loose on earth will be loosed in heaven.

Matthew 16: 19

A prayer

Lord, you should be very careful who you give your keys to. Wasn't that a little on the naive side? . . . Well yes, I realize that the keys come with responsibilities, and they're not just for opening the doors that suit yourself. But, did I ever tell you, you are a very generous and trusting Lord? Just give me a minute while I figure out what all these keys are for. Amen

Putting down roots

To continue the theme of building the church: Jonathan Sacks, the Chief Rabbi, also mentions in *The Home We Build Together* another parable. This time it is about 100 strangers who find themselves in the middle of a big city. There they find a hotel which is large, comfortable and has every amenity. The visitors have enough money to pay their hotel bills. They book their rooms, unpack and stay. The rules are very simple. They are free to do what they like as long as they don't disturb the other guests. They pay money in return for certain services, keep an eye out to see whether other hotels charge less or offer more, but by and large are satisfied with where they are.

The church we build is not a hotel. A hotel is really just a place to stay for a while. You have no roots there. It's just a gathering of strangers who are there out of a sense of shared convenience. You might say hello to one another, talk about the weather and the football. But ultimately you are still strangers.

The church Jesus builds in us is more than that. The cliché is to say it is a place where strangers become friends. But even that is not enough. The church Jesus builds in us is something with an identity, and a purpose, which draws people into a sense of being 'in this together'. Making that identity and purpose clear, and helping each other to own it, are essential parts of building the church of Christ.

Building a church which loves our neighbours

Be under obligation to no one – the only obligation you have is to love one another. Whoever does this has obeyed the Law. The commandments: Do not commit adultery; do not commit murder; do not steal; do not desire what belongs to someone else – all these, and any others besides, are summed up in the one command, Love your neighbour as you love yourself. If you love others, you will never do them wrong; to love, then, is to obey the whole Law.

You must do this, because you know that the time has come for you to wake up from your sleep.

Romans 13: 8–11

A prayer

Lord, it's easy nowadays to be blasé about neighbours. Neighbourhoods have changed, and we don't know each other like earlier generations did. So, you have a lot to work out in us. Build us into a church which values, recognizes, seeks out and loves our neighbours. Amen

Let us do this together

Jonathan Sacks, in his book *The Home We Build Together*, has furnished me with a third and final parable: 100 strangers arrive at a town. There they are met by the mayor, councillors and local residents. The mayor says, Friends we welcome you. It is good to have you among us. Sadly as you can see there is no country house where we might accommodate you. Nor do we have a hotel. There is, though, something else we can offer.

We have a patch of empty land: large enough to accommodate homes for all of you. We have bricks and building materials. We have experts here who can help you design your homes, and we will help you build them. Meanwhile we will offer you hospitality while the homes are being built. Let us do this together.

If you apply that parable to the way in which we build the church, it is quite demanding. The newcomers don't have to earn their place by being there a minimum length of time. They are not guests. They are brought in to work with those who are already there to build something new. They are not left entirely to their own devices; they are treated as full partners in the work Christ has called us to do.

The church we build – and remember we are not talking property schemes here – is the church we build together.

Jesus gives a new status to his people

You are my friends if you do what I command you. No longer do I call you servants, for the servant does not know what his master is doing; but I have called you friends, for all that I have heard from my Father I have made known to you. You did not choose me, but I chose you . . .

John 15: 14–16

A prayer

Lord, I suppose I'd prefer to think that I have chosen to follow you. But before I did that you had been working in my life – and others' too. Thank you for that. And Lord, as you build your church in us, may that sense of grace characterize our behaviour and friendships. Enable us to live, together, as those who are your friends. Amen

Half a shekel each

The Word became a human being and, full of grace and truth, lived among us. Those words from John 1 are among the most famous in the Bible. To be honest 'lived among us' is not as graphic as the original Greek. It really means Jesus *pitched his tent among us.*

The Tent in the Old Testament was something you carried with you. It is described in meticulous detail in Exodus 26–40. It was a fairly sizeable tent, lavishly decorated. It symbolized God's presence when the people of Israel were on their journey to the Promised Land. And it lay right in the middle of the camp, like a public square. It wasn't built by a couple of professional tent-makers. All the Israelites contributed to it. Some brought gold, others silver or bronze. Some brought curtains, skins, or wood. Others brought their time and skills. Everyone was asked to contribute half a shekel – the rich not more, the poor not less.

Perhaps building that Tent together did more than anything else to give the Israelites their peculiar identity as being a people. It focused on valuing everyone without exception; it focused on the future; it focused on the God whose presence was to be found in its very centre.

Jesus pitched his Tent among us. A new focus for God's purposes, for God's presence among us. Summoning together the gifts of those who would follow him. That Tent is still a good model for building the church. It's not something for a few. Building the church is something we are all called to be involved in. It takes a lot of grace and it takes a lot of truth.

Rebuilding

So we went on rebuilding the wall, and soon it was half its full height because the people were eager to work.

Nehemiah 4: 6

A prayer

Lord, sometimes building or rebuilding seems impossible. And yet, Lord, with you all things are possible. For you have pitched your tent among us. You have pitched in with us big time. Give us that grace to to work together and shape us not just into busy churches but into a real people. Amen

Obedience has its limits

You would think, wouldn't you, that a language that was so keen on commandments would have the word 'obey' in its repertoire of words. The language of the Old Testament was Hebrew. The commandments tot up to 613 in number. But there is no word for 'obey'. Instead you get a word that means listen, attend, understand, respond. When King James' men were translating the Bible they had to come up with a new word to get the meaning of the Hebrew across: *hearken.*

If someone asked you to name an obedient character in the Old Testament you might think of Noah. When God told him to build an ark he didn't say a word; he just got on with it. But it makes you wonder whether that was quite the response God wanted. Would it not have been better to challenge God and the need for the Flood? And why didn't Noah press God to save more than just his family? Noah might have been obedient but he may have actually have missed the plot.

At the end of the day God is interested in more than our obedience. You can be blindly obedient to God and yet not know him. He might just be more bothered about whether we actually listen to him, really listen, attend, understand, then respond as those who truly know him. Hearken up, chaps! More about Noah next week.

Jesus and the two sisters

As Jesus and his disciples were on their way, he came to a village where a woman named Martha opened her home to him. She had a sister called Mary, who sat at the Lord's feet listening to what he said. But Martha was distracted by all the preparations that had to be made. She came to him and asked, 'Lord, don't you care that my sister has left me to do the work by myself? Tell her to help me!'

Luke 10: 38–40

A prayer

Lord, forgive me when being a good person, doing the right thing, and being swamped with things to do, become an excuse for not listening to you. That may of course be because I am afraid I might find that what you are really saying is not what I want to hear. Are you sure you wouldn't settle for a little more obedience? Amen

Falling apart at the seams

It's always sad to see a once great man fall apart at the seams. That's what happens to Noah in the Old Testament. God singles him out for a special task with the Ark, but he ends up drunk, with no self-respect and an embarrassment to his family. Maybe he had what might be termed today 'survivor's guilt'. Why had he been saved and so many others died? Could he not have done more to help them?

There were already some aspects of his behaviour on the Ark that raise questions. When the Flood recedes and the Ark comes to rest Noah seems to delay leaving the Ark an inordinate amount of time. It makes you wonder when God finally told him to get out, whether he was losing patience with him. It's almost as if Noah had been comfortable (for a while at least) with the notion of building the Ark. But then he finds himself shrinking back from the next phase. The world as he knew it was no more. The task now was to build a new one.

When things around you fall apart at the seams what is needed is courage, healing and the determination to build something new. It may well be that Noah failed that particular challenge – and he ended up falling apart at the seams himself. A cautionary tale!

Jesus leaves 'the Ark'

Jesus and his disciples went on to the villages around Caesarea Philippi [*where they had been saving others, not just themselves*]. *On the way he asked them, 'Who do people say I am?' They replied, 'Some say John the Baptist; others say Elijah; and still others, one of the prophets.' 'But what about you?' he asked. 'Who do you say I am?' Peter answered, 'You are the Messiah'* [*recognizing that a new and more demanding phase was in front of them*]. *Jesus warned them not to tell anyone about him.*

Mark 8: 27–30 [My notes in brackets]

A prayer

Lord, it's hard not to feel some sympathy for Noah. Maybe you asked too much of him. Or maybe he didn't ask enough of you? Lord, give us the wisdom to know when to move on, the determination to do it, the grace to cope with the sacrifice involved, and the joy of knowing we are building your kingdom. Amen

You are now a hero

When my brother joined the Fire Service all the new recruits were given a pep talk: *You are now a hero.* Part of their job was to save the lives of other people. And the clear implication was: take that seriously. The problem with Noah is that while he was a good and righteous man, he was no hero. He saved himself and his family, and of course the animals. But he didn't save anyone else. Compared to someone like Moses, who brought all his people from their captivity in Egypt to a life of freedom, Noah comes off badly. He was no hero.

One of the terms we use in our Christian vocabulary is *outreach.* We reach out in the name of God to other people. That might be in prayer; it might be in forgiveness; it might be with hope and expectation; it might be reaching out in a whole host of practical ways. Our outreach should be clear, focused, and if it is to have Christian integrity it must reach out beyond ourselves.

Jesus reached out in extraordinary ways to a far wider range of people that would have stretched even the most accomplished of heroes. He was in the business of saving others. Listen up, those of you in Jesus' service: *You are now a hero.* That's something to be taken seriously. Note the touch of irony in the last sentence of the reading below.

Jesus reaches out in ways others cannot comprehend

They crucified two rebels with him, one on his right and one on his left. Those who passed by hurled insults at him, shaking their heads and saying, 'So! You who are going to destroy the temple and build it in three days, come down from the cross and save yourself!' In the same way the chief priests and the teachers of the law mocked him among themselves. 'He saved others,' they said, 'but he can't save himself!'

Mark 15: 27–31

A prayer

Lord, you saved others. I am glad you did, and you did that in some fantastic ways. Now I have got some people on my mind whose lives could do with being made more whole and complete. You know who they are already but I'm going to tell you anyway, because they mean a lot to me: . . . Lord, today I trust you reach out to them. Help us to reach out as generously as you did. Amen

Please, sir, it was me!

I like the Jewish story about the Rabbi who was teaching his class about Joshua. He asked Samuel at the back of the class: *Who destroyed the walls of Jericho*? Samuel replied: *Please, sir, it wasn't me!* The Rabbi mentioned this to Samuel's parents and they said rather indignantly: *If Samuel said it wasn't him, then it wasn't him.* He told the President of the synagogue this sad state of affairs. The President listened, opened his drawer and then wrote a cheque, saying. *Here's some money. Get the walls repaired and stop complaining.*

The story illustrates how reluctant we often are to accept responsibility. *Please, sir, it wasn't me.* So your church is going through a tough time. The congregations are smaller; the Ministers are thinly stretched. Key people get ill, move house or sadly die. Or the walls don't get repaired. You can blame the difficulties on things that happened in the past, the changes the world has gone through in the past 50 years. You can blame things on particular people, the weather, or even God.

Or you can accept responsibility yourself. Not for the past, necessarily. But for the future. You do that, whenever you hear God's call and respond. Remember that woman who once touched Jesus' clothes in the hope that she might be cured. Jesus turned round, notices that something had gone out of him, and asked who it was. Her response might be paraphrased: *Please, sir, it was me!*

Abraham hears the call of God

The Lord had said to Abram, 'Go from your country, your people and your father's household to the land I will show you. 'I will make you into a great nation, and I will bless you; I will make your name great, and you will be a blessing . . . So Abram went, as the Lord had told him; and Lot went with him. Abram was seventy-five years old when he set out from Haran.

Genesis 12: 1, 2, 4

A prayer

Lord, today we turn to you not as victims of circumstances beyond our control. We turn to you as those whom you have called to be disciples. Help us to create a new future in Jesus' name. Amen

The capacity to change

They will never change! How often have we heard that! And is that really true? I recently read the account of a Korean Airlines plane crash that happened in 1997, and in which 73 of the 158 passengers died. There was no one cause, but a minor technical malfunction, bad weather and a tired pilot, which all combined to create a scenario where everyone in the cockpit needed to work together. And that didn't happen.

It didn't happen because of Korean culture. How you speak to someone else in Korean depends on your relative standing or status. A first officer couldn't tell the pilot he had overlooked something. The best he could do was to offer a veiled hint, even when he knew a crash was imminent. In fact Korean Airlines were statistically significantly more vulnerable to air accidents than many other airlines. People might well have looked at Korean culture and said: *They will never change!*

Korean Airlines is now one of the safest airlines in the world. They might not be able to change Korean culture in its entirety but they did change the culture of the cockpit so pilots and crew could operate as a proper team.

In our churches there are some things we do need to change – and I will discuss four this month – and if we don't, the consequences may also be catastrophic. Maybe God is asking us to look at the culture within our churches and make the changes we need to. Never underestimate people's capacity for change!

Paul addresses a problem in the culture of the Church at Corinth

When you come together, it is not really to eat the Lord's Supper. For when the time comes to eat, each of you goes ahead with your own supper, and one goes hungry and another becomes drunk. What!

I Corinthians 11: 20–21

A prayer

Lord, I know there is no reason why change shouldn't happen, but you do realize, don't you, that in practice people are just too tired, too set in their ways – or both. Yes, you have high expectations and some people did change – Paul, Zacchaeus, the Prodigal Son. But surely they were exceptions, were't they? All right, models then. You'd better raise our levels of expectation as a matter of priority. Amen

Putting the club to bed

Many years ago I went one Sunday to a church in London called Clubland Methodist Church. It was largely a black church and I can still remember a few things about the service. The Minister asked a young black man to speak – he spoke off the cuff, brilliantly, for a few minutes on community affairs. Years later I saw him again on television when he was in national politics. When they shared the peace it took ages; everyone greeted everyone. When they read the Bible they took turns. You didn't opt in to read; you opted out. If someone wasn't a natural reader it really didn't matter. People listened intently anyway.

Despite its name, this church was not a club. A club exists primarily for the benefit of its own members (though there are notable exceptions). A church is something different. It looks beyond its members. Beyond even the community it professes to serve. It looks to the living God, and recognizes his character in the way Jesus lived his life and taught his disciples. And more than that, it sometimes waits, sometimes acts, sometimes loves as if that living God is blowing in its sails.

It's our vision of God that changes our perception of ourselves, one another, our community and ultimately our world. If we have lost our sense of vision, or lost confidence in that vision, then we are heading backwards into being a club. And that is an awfully dangerous place to be. As Proverbs (29: 18) says: without vision the people perish.

Jesus talks of a God who expects a bit more

If you love those who love you, what credit is that to you? Even sinners love those who love them. And if you do good to those who are good to you, what credit is that to you? Even sinners do that. And if you lend to those from whom you expect repayment, what credit is that to you? Even sinners lend to sinners, expecting to be repaid in full. But love your enemies, do good to them, and lend to them without expecting to get anything back.

Luke 6: 32–35

A prayer

Lord, today we turn to you not as victims of circumstances beyond our control. We turn to you as those whom you have called to be disciples. I think we need not just vision but the determination to make the vision come alive. Amen

Who is responsible for worship?

There is something about our perception of worship that needs to change. *Who is responsible for worship in your church?* It is easy to point to particular individuals who have certain roles. There is the Minister or Local Preacher who will be leading worship; there may be a worship leader. Then there is the Church Steward who contacts the preacher in advance and gets everything ready. Not to mention the Organist who has been trying to get to grips with new tunes. Oh, and there are those who put the flowers in, welcome people at the door, choirs and music groups, and those who provide refreshments afterwards. They are all responsible for worship, you will say.

Of course all those people have very important roles. But we will have far more vibrant worship when every member of the congregation answers that simple question – who is responsible for worship in your church? – with two words: *I am.*

Just think – *you* are responsible (along with everyone else) for the atmosphere in worship, and for making newcomers welcome. You are responsible for encouraging those that participate, praying for the service in advance, expressing your appreciation for the Local Preacher who has put in hours of preparation. You are responsible for whether our focus is on God or on ourselves. You are responsible for being there and encouraging others to celebrate our faith there, too. You may not actively take a leading role in worship. But you can bring out the best in those that do. That's more of a change in our culture than you might realize.

Encouragement from Paul

Finally, brothers and sisters, whatever is true, whatever is noble, whatever is right, whatever is pure, whatever is lovely, whatever is admirable – if anything is excellent or praiseworthy – think about such things. Whatever you have learned or received or heard from me, or seen in me – put it into practice. And the God of peace will be with you.

Philippians 4: 8–9

A prayer

Lord, forgive me when I have left things to everyone else. Lord, help me to make our worship fit for a King. Amen

The eccentric tutor

When I was training for the ministry and studying the New Testament we had a very eccentric tutor. However, amongst his gifts was getting us all to participate in Bible Study. We would sit in a circle and read the particular passage we were looking at. No-one was allowed to say too much. We went around in a circle and everyone was asked in turn to make a small contribution to the session.

You could make a comment – That surprised me . . . That reminds me of . . . She has got a lot more faith than I would have.

Or you could ask a question. Could someone explain what that means? Why would Jesus do that?

Invariably discussion would soon follow.

It wasn't intimidating and it certainly wasn't rocket science. No-one was made to feel ignorant, and those who were 'full of it' were kept in check! And we had some really fascinating and interesting sessions.

In many of our churches we have got out of the habit of house groups, cell groups, whatever we call them. But being a part of a small group that meets to share and discuss our faith is an important part of how we grow – in more ways than one. That might be something we need to address. My old tutor would think we were rather eccentric for letting small groups disappear from the scene.

Paul shares his faith

I'm not ashamed of the gospel: it is God's own power for salvation to all who have faith in God, to the Jew first and also to the Greek. God's righteousness is being revealed in the gospel, from faithfulness for faith, as it is written, The righteous person will live by faith.

Romans 1: 16–17

A prayer

Lord, why is it that some parts of the Bible are straightforward, and the other bits were written by St Paul? Almost as if you were trying to pull us together, so we don't try to be solo Christians. Lord you give us the opportunities to share and explore our faith. Give us the will to make things happen. Amen

The 10,000-hour rule

A study was done in the 1990s at an elite musical academy in Berlin. They wondered whether there were any natural talents who could rise effortlessly to the top without putting in the hours of practice the others did. There weren't.

Most of the violinists had started at the same age and practised the same sort of hours when they were young. But by the time they were 20 there were roughly three groups: those who had practised 4,000 hours, those who had practised 8,000 hours, those who had practised 10,000 hours. This corresponded roughly to those who would become music teachers, good performers, and world-class soloists respectively.

Apparently this 10,000-hour rule as a recipe for excellence can be transferred widely across a number of fields. I wondered how it would be for Jesus. His ministry lasted three years from his baptism to his crucifixion. 912 days (2.5 years) x 12 (working hours each day) = 10,950. That takes us more or less to the point where Jesus 'set his face to Jerusalem' and the cross.

Did Jesus expect the same of his followers? Yes and No. Those who had long hours of Christian experience he expected great things of. But he also valued immensely those who had little.

Jesus saying Yes

Have I been with you all this time, Philip, and you still do not know me?

John 14: 9

Jesus saying No

Truly, I tell you, unless you change and become like children you will never enter the kingdom of heaven.

Matthew 18: 3

A prayer

Lord, just to let you know I have probably been practising my faith well over 10,000 hours and I am still trying to play the notes in the right order. I need you to help me speak, see and live as one who has known you a long time. And to help me take on board what you say with the faith and joy of someone who has met you for the first time. Oh, and Lord, thanks for putting in the practice. Amen

The ministry of reconciliation

A personal note: My daughter now lives in Australia. We text, email or talk most days and I'd like to think we have a pretty good relationship. She wears her heart on her sleeve and frequently tells me how excited she is at the prospect of Joanna and me visiting her next year. We plan to do that as part of my Sabbatical.

It's not always been like that. There was a time when we didn't speak for over a year. I learned afterwards that she was being pressured into taking legal steps so that I could never speak to her again. Why is not really that important. But, she says, she was on the brink of the worst decision of her life.

One day I had to contact her. My mother was terminally ill in hospital and I told her that if she wanted to see her Grandma again now was the time to go. My mother had always been good at bringing people together, and that gift now even extended to when she was unconscious. Seeing her jolted my daughter into stepping back from the brink. Life was too short to hold grudges, real or imagined. More than that, it launched her into the very positive step of wanting to re-establish not a passable relationship with her father but a very good one.

My mother exercised a ministry of reconciliation. It's a ministry St Paul says we have all been entrusted with, and one which I would like to explore this month.

Therefore, if anyone is in Christ, the new creation has come: The old has gone, the new is here! All this is from God, who reconciled us to himself through Christ and gave us the ministry of reconciliation: that God was reconciling the world to himself in Christ, not counting people's sins against them. And he has committed to us the message of reconciliation.

2 Corinthians 5: 17–19

A prayer

Lord, fancy not counting my sins against me! It's very easy to count up the things people do to you. You wouldn't believe how good some people are at arithmetic. But you don't, do you? Count, I mean. I can't imagine you don't think that those sins don't matter. It's just that it's never stopped you loving us – big time. That counts for a lot. Amen

When reconciliation is tough

A pastoral note: I am writing about the ministry of reconciliation this month and I know that for many of you this is a painful subject. Marriages and other relationships sometimes do break down and cannot always be put back together. Even if we have the energy, the will and desire for reconciliation, it needs the same from others too – and then some! This is not about making people feel guilty or at fault for those times when reconciliation has not happened. It's about releasing hope.

Whenever reconciliation takes place – whether between individuals, groups, churches or nations – it's usually because something new has happened. Someone said sorry, offered a handshake, made a journey, or did something totally unexpected. Maybe they came to see someone else in a new light. Or someone lifted the chips off their shoulder and showed them how they could be different.

Reconciliation may not always happen. It may only get so far. It may be complete. But it can only happen when someone decides they are going to be, in effect, the 'something new' that happens. Jesus, of course, did that in a rather unique way.

From Jesus' Sermon on the Mount

Therefore, if you are offering your gift at the altar and there remember that your brother or sister has something against you, leave your gift there in front of the altar. First go and be reconciled to them; then come and offer your gift

Matthew 5: 23–24

A prayer

Lord, it isn't that easy you know. Sometimes they are just so unreasonable. I shouldn't say it, but they are downright un-Christian. If I take you literally and I have to be reconciled with them first, there may not be anything in the collection plate for quite some while. And they may not actually change! Would it be all right if I just prayed for them first for a bit? Amen

It will never work here

In April 2012 a remarkable man died. He was Ray Davey, 97, and the founder of the Corrymeela Community in Northern Ireland. He wanted to bring together people from different backgrounds and cultures and to help them find there are more effective ways than violence to solve their differences. It has been a remarkable ministry of reconciliation.

One of the many things Corrymeela has done is to set up what is called the *The Forgiveness Education Programme* in Primary Schools. Children learn how kindness, generosity and caring can help them understand what forgiveness is about. They also learn that forgiving is not about forgetting what has happened. Instead, it is about learning to remember and tell the story of the past in a new kind of way.

Maybe it's not only primary school children and Irish Protestants and Catholics that need to learn that. Let's be honest, some of our Methodist churches could do with a bit of reconciling. Not that we have been tempted to turn to violence. Mutual antipathy and disregard have been more than sufficient.

It's time to pick up the ministry of reconciliation with which we have been entrusted. *It will never work here.* Really? Ask Ray Davey. Or, at least, the community he has bequeathed.

Truly, I tell you, unless you change and become like children you will never enter the kingdom of heaven.

Matthew 18: 3

A prayer

Lord, have you ever had that feeling, that tinge of excitement, that moment of awakening and you can't wait to get something done . . . then you put the covers back over your head and go back to sleep again? No? Well that's probably because you are God. Well, it happens a lot to some of us. Lord, help us make your dreams our dreams, and help us to make them a reality. Amen

An unexpected donor

The Israeli–Palestinian conflict has been going on for a long time. Its roots are complex and the differences have been as profound as the protagonists have been intransigent. Maybe one day there will be an agreement around a table, but that can only happen when some of the pieces, the fragments of reconciliation have already been put in place. Let me tell you of one of those pieces.

In September 2002, a 7-year-old Palestinian girl from East Jerusalem was waiting for a kidney transplant. She had been on dialysis for two years. That same month a suicide bomber unleashed 15 pounds of explosive on a bus in Tel Aviv. One of the victims was a 19-year-old Scot, a brilliant student and a Jew destined, so it seemed, for a bright career as a doctor. The explosion left him brain-dead. He was in intensive care but there was no hope.

His family came to the decision that as his prime motivation in life was to save others they would offer his kidneys, liver and spleen for transplant surgery. One 7-year-old girl – and it had been one of her people who had killed this young man – was among those whose life was changed that day.[1]

That was quite an act, a remarkably courageous gesture from that Jewish family. It's one thing to think you might act in a certain way in principle. But when it happens to you and your family it isn't that easy. A ministry of reconciliation is not easy. But all of those fragments add up. What we declare is that the actions of another young Jewish man 2,000 years ago actually epitomise the reconciling love of God.

Jesus said

My command is this: Love each other as I have loved you. Greater love has no one than this: to lay down one's life for one's friends. You are my friends if you do what I command.

John 15: 12–14

A prayer

Lord, that kind of generosity and courage is profoundly humbling. I thank you that you have raised up people of faith – of whatever kind – and who can live like that. I also find it just as humbling, Lord, that you should have entrusted your ministry of reconciliation to such as us. Amen

[1] Jonathan Sacks (2005) *To Heal a Fractured World: The Ethics of Responsibility* (London: Schocken Books).

The one thing that's missing

An expert in diamonds was once on a plane and sitting next to him was an elegant woman wearing the largest, most stunning diamond ring he had ever seen. He told her he was in the diamond business and would love to know more about it.

'Well, I am Mrs Klopman', she said 'and this is the Klopman Diamond. It is beautiful, isn't it?'

The expert was indeed overwhelmed by its lustre and beauty.

'Unfortunately', she added, 'there is a terrible curse attached to it.'

The man was intrigued. 'Oh, and what might that be?'

'Mr. Klopman.'

It's an old Yiddish story that has been around for decades. The things we possess can be both a blessing and a curse. We can enjoy them, share them, even wear them. But spare a thought for poor Mrs Klopman, trapped between her love of her possessions and her desire to be free.

Jesus once met a rich young man, who actually had much to commend him. There is just one thing missing, Jesus said. And that is always the rub – dealing with the one thing in your life, or your church, that is missing. Holding onto the diamonds – or Mr Klopman – might be easier.

Jesus said

'If you want to be perfect, go, sell your possessions and give to the poor, and you will have treasure in heaven. Then come, follow me.' When the young man heard this, he went away sad, because he had great wealth.

Matthew 19: 21–22

A prayer

Lord, if you are looking for people to be perfect before they follow you, the queue is going to be very short. Besides which, I am not sure I want to be perfect. Wouldn't being 'moderately good' do? I understand, mind you, that you want me to deal with the things that are missing. I want to deal with the things that are missing, too. How much, you are asking me? That's the rub, isn't it? Ask me again tomorrow. Amen

Remembering and making peace

There was once an argument that broke out between two Jewish rabbis. In their debates Rabbi Yehuda usually won, and Rabbi Meir usually lost. The one exception was when they were debating some words from the book of Deuteronomy: 'You are children of the Lord your God.'

Rabbi Yehuda reckoned that there were occasions – and as it is Remembrance Day today, you might well think of some – when people have acted in such an awful or brutal way that they lose the right to be called God's children. Rabbi Meir disagreed, and argued that, even when we are at our worst, we remain children of God, no matter how we behave. In this matter, Jewish law sided with Rabbi Meir. We are called God's children; we remain God's children, at all times and in all places.

Jesus was often called 'Rabbi'. I wonder where he would have stood in the argument. I suspect he would have been sympathetic towards Rabbi Meir in many ways. You are a child of God and you can't lose God's love for you – no matter what. But I suspect Jesus wanted to go beyond the issue as to whether being a child of God was a status you could keep or lose. It was also a calling you chose. One way of answering that call was to become a peacemaker. Making peace is much more difficult than making war. Perhaps it is not an accident that when Jesus said *Blessed are the peacemakers* he also added *for they shall become children of God.*

To remember without making peace incites only hatred and vengeance. To remember and make peace renews our place as God's children and out of a curse he produces a blessing.

You are children of the Lord your God.

Deuteronomy 14: 1

Blessed are the peacemakers, for they will be called children of God

Matthew 5: 9

A prayer

Lord, making peace with people is hard, especially when you have left it too late. Making peace between people is even harder. But today is a day for remembrance and I will remember your call to be a peacemaker. Make me a channel of your peace. Make me one of your children. Amen

God bless you!

God bless you! Now there's a well-worn pious phrase. In the course of my ministry I have been asked to bless all sorts of things – food, homes, marriages, pets, rosary beads, hymn books, boats, even bingo nights. I have heard *God bless you!* as a way of giving thanks, or as a prayer of protection as someone goes away. The connection with sneezing goes back to at least 77 AD, though despite all sorts of imaginative suggestions, no-one really knows why.

But what is blessing about? It first appears in the creation story. The creation story does not flow uninterrupted. Three times God stops – to bless living creatures, then humankind, then a day of rest [Genesis 1: 22, 28; 2: 3]. As if to say: I don't want you just to exist; I want you to have a life that is full and overflowing.

Blessing other people is not about giving them a dose of religion. It's about wanting them to have the full lives God intended for them. And there's a sense of gratitude for who they are and the roles they have played that a blessing brings with it, too.

We also bless God: *Bless the Lord, O my soul* [Psalm 103]. It's a shorthand way of saying: Lord, you are the source of my life, and when I trust you, you rescue me from the curses of anxiety, arrogance and despair. Blessing, whether of people, places or God, can be our way of interrupting what we are doing to make life sing.

God bless you!

Jesus said

I have come that they may have life in all its fullness.

John 10: 10

A prayer

Lord, so you came and interrupted people's lives – on the sea-shore, in the market place and in the synagogue! You gave people a sense that their lives mattered much more than they ever imagined. Thank you for interrupting my life today. Bless the Lord, O my soul! Amen

Blessing the insufferable

You may have heard of Corrie ten Boom. She was a Dutch Christian who harboured Jews during World War II to prevent them being sent to the concentration camps. Eventually she was arrested and sent to Ravensbrück herself. Later, at a church service in Munich, she met and shook hands with a former prison guard from the camp where her family was killed. That was not easy and the memories of guards mocking them, and the pale face of her sister came flooding back. Overcoming all her instincts she took his hand and then a current seemed to pass down her shoulder through her hand to his. Hatred had turned to love.

In the Sermon on the Mount, Jesus asked those who were listening to do something that went against all their natural instincts: *Bless those who curse you.*

It's easy to curse people. Following people who are driving unreasonably slowly can be very frustrating. Standing in a queue at the Post Office for one stamp while the lady in front has 17 parcels and then insists on regaling the person behind the counter with a further instalment of her many ailments, trials and tribulations does tend to make blood boil. As for people selling PPI insurance . . .

Blessing people who stand in your way or who offend you, hurt you or stand for everything you despise is quite a task. Well, Jesus never said it was easy.

Jesus said [on the Cross]

Father, forgive them, for they don't know what they are doing.

Luke 23: 34

A prayer

Lord, how can you say they didn't know what they were doing? They knew very well. They just didn't care, or were just following orders, or they just accepted this was something they couldn't change. But don't tell me they didn't know what they were doing. Don't absolve them from their responsibilities. Or is it that you thought they don't know the whole picture, or didn't know what *you* were doing? What surprises me is that whenever I hear those words of yours from the cross I feel a strange current coming through my hand. Amen

The sounds we filter out

One of the faculties we as human beings have developed is the capacity to screen out certain sounds. When I was a student at Durham, I lived no more than a stone's throw from Durham Cathedral. When I first went there, the noise of the bells chiming the hours was unmissable. But it didn't last. Visitors would come and say, 'How do you manage to sleep through that?' The reality was that I soon did not even notice the bells. I screened them out. I suspect people who live near airports, busy roads and railway lines might say much the same sort of thing.

There can be occasions though when we attune our ears to certain sounds. Even when we were asleep there was a part of us still listening to any untoward sounds from the baby in the next room or for the door opening when a son or daughter might be returning from a late night out.

Advent is listening time. We shall be listening to stories so familiar we might screen them out without even noticing. Or we filter them as children's stories without recognizing that they may contain untoward sounds we do well to listen out for.

How then can we listen? One possibility when you say your prayers in Advent is to begin them with an unfamiliar sound – a bell, a (saucepan) gong, or the tapping of your fingers to a particular tune you choose. It may well be that those same sounds interrupt you some time – a time you didn't expect or choose. But then you never know what is going to happen when God is doing his stuff.

A distinctive note

Even in the case of lifeless things that make sounds, such as the pipe or harp, how will anyone know what tune is being played unless there is a distinction in the notes?

1 Corinthians 14: 7

A prayer

Lord, you know how I react to those jarring sounds – the unrestrained shout up the street, the dee-dah of the ambulance, the music I do not care for or understand, the voice of someone I find difficult – well help me when I listen to you to to react positively. Amen

Why wouldn't God want to deal with you?

There were once two women who quite independently had had similar experiences. Both were expecting children, though one was young and the other had long since given up hope of conceiving. Each felt that there was a religious dimension to their experience. And, by chance or otherwise, they met up. In fact they spent the next three months together supporting one another.

No prizes for guessing, but they were of course Mary, Jesus' mother, and Elizabeth, the mother of John the Baptist. Now their time together may just have been incidental, but my guess is that it was quite significant. I have met several people who wondered at first whether their experience of God was genuine or illusory. Was that an answer to prayer? Was that a coincidence? Why would God speak to the likes of me? And, left to their own devices, their doubts might have overwhelmed them.

Now Mary and Elizabeth might conceivably – no pun intended – have egged each other on, but their story is not told in that way. They simply supported one another. They came together around a promise that, through the children they were expecting, God was going to do some extraordinary things. That they met up might well have made all the difference.

Advent is trusting time. Time to trust your own experience, time to trust your own experience of God, time to trust God. Why wouldn't God want to deal with you? It's a time to support one another as we all gather round that same promise – that God is with us in a remarkable and unique way.

Elizabeth said to Mary

Blessed is she who believed that the promise made by the Lord would be fulfilled.

Luke 1: 45

A prayer

Lord, I can understand that there are some people you would want to deal with. They have talents and gifts I haven't got. They understand things I don't. Their faces fit. I am just me. But I know you hear my prayers. And there are moments when I feel I have heard your voice, too. That's what astonishes me. That's what makes me want to 'magnify my Lord'. Amen

Gaudete Day

Passion comes in many forms. There are the frustrated angry outbursts of inconvenienced Victor Meldrews. There is the note of restrained passion of those who instinctively know something is wrong. Last week someone asked me what I thought of the Church of England's decision not to accept women as bishops. I don't think he was particularly interested in my opinion. He just wanted to say that his children had been baptized by a woman and he had been very impressed. And he felt that his vicar had been badly let down.

Then there is a more unfettered passion. Advent contains that kind of passion. It's a time when we listen to stories that encapsulate God's desire for people to be free – free from all the things that can diminish and enslave them. We see God not complaining, not just registering dissent, but deciding to be a force that puts things right.

In certain churches this is called *Gaudete* Day. *Gaudete* is an unrestrained and passionate word that means *Rejoice*! Where they normally light purple candles in church in Advent, on this day it's a pink one. It's a joyful passionate note. Be glad because the kind of God we have is a passionate God. That's what lay at the heart of Jesus' ministry. Time for us to be passionate, to respond to the Gospel in a way that causes God and others, especially those who have been passed over, to rejoice, too.

From Mary's song

He has brought down rulers from their thrones
  but has lifted up the humble.
He has filled the hungry with good things
  but has sent the rich away empty.

Luke 1: 52–53

A prayer

Lord, I thank you that you are not only the God of passion, compassion and justice, but that with you there is also a sense of joy and delight. I thank you that Mary caught that, and I pray that I will catch it too. Amen

Shepherds

I like watching Professor Brian Cox on television. He is a brilliant scientist, an engaging personality and a very able communicator. You listen to his explanations of the mysteries at the heart of the universe, you marvel, and you even feel for a moment that you even understand it. The moment usually passes quickly for me.

There are some mysteries though that not even the greatest minds can penetrate. One such is what was actually going on in the birth of Jesus, that mysterious thing we call the incarnation, or as Charles Wesley put it more poetically:

Our God contracted to a span,
Incomprehensibly made Man.

Now you can, if you are clever enough, devote yourself to trying to get your head around that mystery. You will never crack it of course, any more than you will work out how to get the waters cascading over Niagara into a teacup. But it has fascinated great minds for centuries.

My favourite characters in the Christmas story have always been the shepherds, those dirt-poor, uneducated young men minding their sheep in the fields around Bethlehem. If you had asked them about the incarnation, you would not have got much sense out of them. But they get drawn into this mystery, simply enjoy it, marvel at the things they have seen and amaze others with their story. Their cup overflows. Don't lose the capacity to be drawn into this mystery, too. That's where you begin.

The Shepherds are drawn in

An angel of the Lord appeared to them, and the glory of the Lord shone around them, and they were terrified. But the angel said to them, 'Do not be afraid. I bring you good news that will cause great joy for all the people. Today in the town of David a Saviour has been born to you; he is the Messiah, the Lord. This will be a sign to you: You will find a baby wrapped in cloths and lying in a manger.'

Luke 2: 9–12

A prayer

Lord, today I want to thank you for those who have applied their minds and creative abilities to such marvellous effect. Thank you for scientists, musicians and stunning television. Thank you for your creative power, the songs of angels, and the images of grace you left us at Bethlehem. Amen

The graveyard slot

There is in the world of television something called the graveyard slot. It's a time when the producers don't expect large audiences. They might put on re-runs of old movies, game shows that never quite made it or public affairs programmes no-one wants to watch anyway.

The Sunday after Christmas may seem like the church's equivalent. The main event is over. Christmas is a few days away and everyone is recovering. Traditionally this Sunday is one of the worst in the year for church attendances. It can feel like the faithful few mopping up after the party is over and everyone has gone home.

If preachers feel they too have been awarded the graveyard slot then that may only be enhanced if they take one of the day's traditional readings. You probably remember the gruesome account in St Matthew's Gospel of the 'slaughter of the innocents' by King Herod. Not the easiest of themes to tackle.

But occasionally the graveyard slot produces something remarkable, and everyone complains they have missed it. Today you might well get the feeling that while the festivities are over the real journey now begins. It will not be without difficulties or, like the slaughter of the innocents, unwelcome even tragic events. But it is a journey that will take us from Bethlehem to Jerusalem, from birth to rebirth when we celebrate the resurrection at Easter. Now there's a graveyard slot to be reckoned with.

Joseph's family journey from Egypt to Galilee

But when he heard that Archelaus was reigning in Judea in place of his father Herod, he was afraid to go there. Having been warned in a dream, he withdrew to the district of Galilee, and he went and lived in a town called Nazareth. So was fulfilled what was said through the prophets, that he would be called a Nazarene.

Matthew 2: 22–23

A prayer

Lord, so you mean the real work now begins. You are on a journey which takes you through your childhood, your education in Nazareth, your training as a carpenter to the day your life changes at the River Jordan. Then you travel in earnest. Lord, you realize this is not a time of great activity on my part, but I just want you to know that on this inauspicious day, that I intend to follow you through the coming year. Can you make sure I don't miss anything important? Amen

A new currency

There are two sides to a bank note. On the front you get (in addition to a picture of the Queen) a promise signed by the Chief Cashier of the Bank of England: 'I promise to pay the bearer on demand the sum of . . .' It's dry stuff which used to mean (up to 1931) you could exchange your note for gold at a bank. Now it just means it's real money. It's probably the side to which we pay most attention.

On the other side there are some extraordinary people – Elizabeth Fry, the prison reformer (£5), Charles Darwin, the naturalist (£10), Adam Smith, the father of economics (£20), and Matthew Boulton and James Watt, manufacturer and designer of steam engines (£50). In their own unique ways they changed people's lives because they glimpsed a different kind of promise – that of a future few others could imagine. Then they did something about it.

Over the next week or two, you may attend a Covenant Service, where we make our annual promises and dedication to God. It sounds as if it's mainly about us. We promise to pay God on demand the sum total of our lives. But it's actually the other side which is much more interesting. The Covenant is about people – Abraham, Moses, John the Baptist, Jesus – who glimpse the promise of something new and seize it.

God's promises add up to a new currency. The person we place the highest value on is Jesus who promised to those who believed in him life in all its fullness. The Cross is the culmination of what he did about it. Another note for your wallet.

A new currency

And my God will meet all your needs according to the riches of his glory in Christ Jesus.

Philippians 4: 19

A prayer

Lord, when I go to the bank and hand over a £10 note I know I am going to get two £5s back. When I promise you something there is a high probability you might get short-changed. Oh, so you know that already. And still you ask me to promise more than I have within me? OK, so where is this going? You want me just to trust more in your promises? Well, you had better help me live within them, then. Amen

When Abram was 99

Amongst my Christmas gifts this year was a novel by a Swedish author named Jonas Jonasson: *The One Hundred Year Old Man Who Climbed Out the Window and Disappeared.* The man in question does not want the fuss and bother of his impending 100th birthday party and he decides to escape the clutches of his old people's home. Numerous escapades follow, and you begin to get a new take on some of the remarkable events of the twentieth century, in which he has apparently played a key role.

It rather flies in the face of the proverbial wisdom that old age is not all it is cracked up to be. Now far be it from me to understate the difficulties many older people face; I simply want to point out that the Christmas celebrations we have recently enjoyed feature older people to no small degree. They too have 'climbed out the window'. There are Elizabeth and Zecharaiah, the parents of John the Baptist. There are the wise men from the east. Then there are Simeon and Anna, the elderly prophetic couple to whom Jesus is brought when he is 8 days old. Clearly, neither God nor life were finished with these people yet. God did not just leave it all to the younger ones (Mary and Joseph)!

I am praying and hoping that this year some significant changes and developments will take place in our churches. And I hope that people of all ages will want to be closely involved. If you consider yourself one of the 'older ones', don't assume God is not interested in you and your gifts. This is a time to climb out of windows – metaphorically speaking!

God speaks to Abraham

When Abram was ninety-nine years old, the Lord appeared to Abram and said to him, 'I am Almighty God; walk before Me and be blameless. And I will make My covenant between Me and you, and will multiply you exceedingly.' Then Abram fell on his face, and God talked with him . . .

Genesis 17: 1–3

A prayer

Lord, I have noticed that you don't care too much for proverbial wisdom. You don't want our horizons limited by the stuff of common experience. I like the idea that Abram was just 99 when you spoke to him. It's a wonderful image of Abram head down in the sand and you just talk to him. Bet he never went to his 100th birthday party either. Amen

Awakenings

One of the most memorable films I have ever seen was called *Awakenings*. It was made in 1990 and starred Robin Williams and Robert de Niro. It features a doctor in New York who was treating some patients who had been in a catatonic state for over 30 years after catching a virus that caused a 'sleeping sickness'. He believes that they are 'alive on the inside' and using a new drug he gets them to awaken. Through music, catching a tennis ball, supported walking, stories, games, and patterns on the floor his patients begin to live again. In fact, they show such a zest for life they remind others of the gifts they have and don't seem to appreciate enough. They want to go dancing, be beautiful, eat their favourite meals and connect with each other. By contrast, the life of the shy but compassionate doctor seems less complete. Sadly the drug's effects don't last and after a couple of months the patients revert to their previous catatonic state.

We may not be in a catatonic state; we do not need drugs; but we are going to have our own programme called *Awakenings* in Lent. It's an opportunity to use more gifts than we usually do in worship. It's a time when we can meet together and share our faith, and ultimately re-awaken our zest for the Gospel of Jesus Christ. It's a time when we allow our compassion and faith to come out on top of our natural reserve.

This programme ends at Easter when we celebrate the ultimate awakening – the resurrection of Jesus. If we start praying about it now, if we are prepared to encourage and bring the best out of each other, then don't be surprised if what is awakened lasts an awful lot longer than two months.

The raising of Jairus' daughter

When they came to the home of the synagogue leader [*Jairus*], *Jesus saw a commotion, with people crying and wailing loudly. He went in and said to them, 'Why all this commotion and wailing? The child is not dead but asleep.' But they laughed at him. After he put them all out, he took the child's father and mother and the disciples who were with him, and went in where the child was. He took her by the hand and said to her, 'Talitha koum!'* (*which means 'Little girl, I say to you, get up!'*)*. Immediately the girl stood up and began to walk around* (*she was twelve years old*)*. At this they were completely astonished.*

Mark 5: 38–42

A prayer

Lord, if you can awaken Jairus' daughter, then awakening me should be a walk in the park. Amen

Lucky Eutychus

The other day I met a dog named Lucky. He belongs to a splendid Christian gentleman I know. Lucky barked when I knocked at the door, checked me over when I sat down, gratefully accepted a bit of fuss and attention and then went to his bed for a sleep while we talked.

It brought to mind an incident that happened in the life of St Paul. He was on the return journey from Greece to Turkey and was staying at a town called Troas. Whether he was preaching, chatting, answering questions or all three, he went on a long time. One young man named Eutychus could not cope. He might well have just come in from a hard day's work and soon fell asleep on the window ledge where he was sitting, and then he fell three stories to the ground. It is not entirely clear whether he was killed or merely knocked unconscious. But Paul picked him up and brought him back to life. Eutychus by the way means 'Lucky'. Never has a Christian been more aptly named.

Well, the door bell rang and Lucky (the dog) was easily awakened and soon demanding to know who else was visiting. There may be times when you think about your own life when you have been 'lucky', too. Lucky to have met certain people, lucky to have found faith in Christ, lucky to have been picked up and brought back to life. It's probably something worth sharing.

Paul, on one of his journeys

Paul spoke to the people and, because he intended to leave the next day, kept on talking until midnight. There were many lamps in the upstairs room where we were meeting. Seated in a window was a young man named Eutychus, who was sinking into a deep sleep as Paul talked on and on. When he was sound asleep, he fell to the ground from the third story and was picked up dead. Paul went down, threw himself on the young man and put his arms around him. 'Don't be alarmed,' he said. 'He's alive!' Then he went upstairs again and broke bread and ate. After talking until daylight, he left. The people took the young man home alive and were greatly comforted.

Acts 20: 7–12

A prayer

Lord, have you noticed when something bad happens that there's always someone who can think how it might have ended up worse, and says: you were lucky! I suppose though that I have been very lucky. In the good times and in the tougher times you have been there to pick me up and bring me to life. You're that kind of God. Amen

Cheeses and the Juice

Rather than typing notes while I have been studying during my Sabbatical, I have experimented with voice recognition software on my computer. I simply dictate the notes and at the press of a button what I have said duly appears on the screen. That's the theory anyway. Now I used to think that I have reasonably clear diction, but I am beginning to think otherwise.

Some of the errors that have appeared on screen are understandable. *Medication* might sound like *meditation. Gymnastic* might sound like *dynastic. Find speeds* could be *finds peace.* Second thoughts began to appear, though, when *the 'I' falls silent* was rendered as *the iPhone 4 is silent* and *faithfulness* had been heard as *Facebook.* The crunch came when I realised my occasional references to *Jesus and the Jews* had all been rendered *Cheeses and the Juice.* I had to decide whether this was really such a good idea after all.

It's not just computers of course that sometimes have difficulty with our language and Christian experience. People can be just the same. The temptation then is simply to speak about our faith only in the places where we can be safely understood. But it may be better simply to persevere until one day we are heard clearly and the penny drops. In the meantime, should the order of service happen to include *Worship the Lord in the beauty of holy nurses* I am sure you will understand.

Paul in Athens (and not overwhelmed)

Paul then stood up in the meeting of the Areopagus and said: 'People of Athens! I see that in every way you are very religious. For as I walked around and looked carefully at your objects of worship, I even found an altar with this inscription: to an unknown god. So you are ignorant of the very thing you worship – and this is what I am going to proclaim to you.'

Acts 17: 22–23

A prayer

Lord, as you well know, finding the right words does not come easily to me. I just ask you to help me find them at the right time, and better still, to live in such a way that the words seem strangely unimportant. Thanks for being the living Word. Amen

The manager's assistant

When the football appears on television, the cameras occasionally focus on the faces of those who are sitting on the bench, particularly the manager. They look for any sign of reaction – whether of delight, anger or frustration. And if he throws his arms up in the air at the referee's blatant bias, or dances a jig when his team scores, it all adds to the entertainment. The manager is the leader. He has ideas, and he stands and falls by the decisions he makes. No wonder he is often excitable.

Next to the manager sits a much calmer figure (well, usually). He's the manager's assistant. He probably deals far more with the players during the week, supervising the training on a daily basis, encouraging them and translating the manager's ideas into action. He lets the manager do the talking on match days, and his gestures are far less dramatic.

A successful team needs both characters. The key figure in the Old Testament was Moses who brought the Israelites out of Egypt towards the Promised Land. He was an inspired prophet. But he also needed his brother Aaron. If Moses had lit a fire in the hearts of his people, it was Aaron who kept the flame burning. Who are those who 'tend the flame' in your church? They might not say much but what they do is vital. Love them.

Tending the flame

In the tent of meeting, outside the curtain that shields the ark of the covenant law, Aaron and his sons are to keep the lamps burning before the Lord from evening till morning. This is to be a lasting ordinance among the Israelites for the generations to come.

Exodus 27: 21

Neither do people light a lamp and put it under a bowl. Instead they put it on its stand, and it gives light to everyone in the house.

Matthew 5: 15

A prayer

Lord, I just thought I would mention that one of the key signs of your grace has always been those people you have placed in my path whose quiet dependability has made all the difference. You can never have enough of them, can you? Amen

Brentford 2, Chelsea 2

As I was driving back from seeing my son in North Wales I was listening to the football commentary on the radio, and the commentator was getting excited. It was the FA Cup 4th round and lowly Brentford had drawn with their mega-rich neighbours Chelsea. Leeds had just beaten Spurs and now goal-shy Oldham were beating Liverpool. 'This is why we love the FA Cup,' he enthused. 'It's so unpredictable!'

Today we begin a journey to Easter that is as unpredictable as you can get. It might not seem so, as we have probably traced that journey many times before, and you know the story. But that sense of unpredictability almost defines the great Biblical journeys. Abraham left behind all the things that made him who he was – his home, his culture, his roots. All because he had a powerful sense that God was calling him. People did not abandon everything just like that and head off Lord knows where. No-one could have predicted that. But it was exciting. Today you will probably hear about Jesus's temptations. A journey was just beginning for him, too. That Jesus was tempted wasn't predictable in the slightest. It was the way he answered those temptations and dealt with them that no-one could have predicted.

If you expect the predictable that's probably what you will get. But if you are open to a God who is sometimes unpredictable, then this Lenten journey may hold a few surprises for you. Sometime shortly after the resurrection I expect there was someone shouting enthusiastically: 'This is why we love God. He is so unpredictable!'

Because he loves me, says the Lord, I will rescue him;
I will protect him, for he acknowledges my name.
He will call on me, and I will answer him;
I will be with him in trouble,
I will deliver him and honour him.

Psalm 91: 14–15

A prayer

Lord, thank goodness you are not unpredictable all the time. I thought for a moment you might be calling to me. I mean you can be predictable *and* faithful, can't you? Ok, so being faithful means we might have to be unpredictable too. Sometimes. Now? Amen

Father Brown

Do you ever get the urge to play detective? Asking questions you might not otherwise have done? Trying to get to the bottom of things? The Father Brown stories have recently been on television, and maybe they have had more of an effect on me than I realised.

The Psalm for today is Psalm 27. As I read it through, I suddenly realized that something must have happened between verse 6 and verse 7. The first six verses talk of a David confident in God and in his faith, almost to the point of being presumptuous. Nothing is going to faze him. God will look after him, no matter what happens. By the time you get to verse 7, David is a much chastened man. Something has happened to leave him frightened and despairing. He has been badly hurt. Maybe he has been humiliated; maybe the political landscape has suddenly changed; maybe he has had a serious illness. His need for God is now a bit different. Some kind of crisis surely has emerged in his life. But what? A case for Father Brown, I suspect.

Jesus, it strikes me, often comes knocking between verses 6 and 7 in our lives. At that moment when our certainties have deserted us, when the steady development of our lives is interrupted by the unexpected, he comes. Today's readings you will find are about people in crisis. When Father Brown has unmasked the culprit it does not end there. He usually helps them to understand the nature of the crisis they are now facing and challenges them about how they are to face it. I wonder where he learned that from.

Jesus meeting the crisis in his own way

At that time some Pharisees came to Jesus and said to him, 'Leave this place and go somewhere else. Herod wants to kill you.' He replied, 'Go tell that fox, "I will keep on driving out demons and healing people today and tomorrow, and on the third day I will reach my goal."'

Luke 13: 31–32

A prayer

Lord, you had a chance there to get out of harm's way and you ignored it. When we come to the critical moments in our lives, I pray that you will be there, too, leading us through, strengthening us and guiding us. Help us to meet those moments in the best way. Amen

Mirror, mirror, on the wall

Should you glimpse my wife at the beginning of a service I am taking you may notice some subtle gestures. These are largely to indicate that my stole is lopsided, the belt on my cassock needs adjusting or my fringe has gone walkabout. A good mirror in the vestry might have helped but churches as a rule do not go a bundle on mirrors, and when they do exist they tend to be rather small or badly positioned.

I suspect mirrors have long been regarded as a sign of vanity and therefore are out of place in church. Mirror, mirror, on the wall, who is the fairest preacher of all? That sort of thing would not do, surely? In an obscure part of Exodus [35: 8] mention is made of a basin and stand in the Temple made out of women's mirrors. According to one tradition, Moses was not too keen about this either. But then, the story goes, he was reminded of the Hebrew slaves who were required to sleep outside where they worked – totally exhausted and with no privacy. The plan was to deter them having more children. However the resourceful women got out their mirrors, made themselves attractive, aroused their husbands, who then fathered more children, thus saving the Jewish people from extinction. Presumably Moses' opinion of mirrors was changed after that.

It's that kind of passionate love that's reflected in today's Psalm. *On my bed I remember you; I think of you through the watches of the night.* [Psalm 63: 6]. It's a mirror image of God's passionate love for us. If there is not enough passion in your church (and sometimes there isn't) a good mirror might not be such a bad thing.

Glimpses of passion in the Old Testament

Love the Lord your God with all your heart and with all your soul and with all your strength.

Deuteronomy 6: 5

I thirst for you, my whole being longs for you, in a dry and parched land where there is no water.

Psalm 63: 1

A prayer

Lord, I am glad that people learned to sing of you with real passion. You are my help, too and I sing in the shadow of your wings. Lord forgive me those things that make my faith and love lukewarm. And make us into communities that will attract others and create hope for a future.

Bell ringing

Some people are reluctant to embrace anything to do with new technology. Not so a certain Roman Catholic priest in Poland. In 2009, he had a high-tech, automated bell system installed in his church. This not only played chimes and gongs very loudly (beginning at 5.00 am) but it also played hymns on a loop system throughout the day. When people in the town complained that their dogs were howling and their children couldn't sleep, the defiant priest simply added another hymn to the loop timed for 1.30 am. He was eventually sentenced to 30 hours community service.

Others are reluctant to embrace older ways of doing things. The Psalm for today is Psalm 32, and it tells of a man who had been reluctant to unburden himself to God and say his prayers. Maybe he felt guilty about something and couldn't talk about it. Maybe he thought that his concerns were too trivial for God to pay any attention to. Eventually he overcame his reluctance and his experience of being forgiven was so overwhelming for him he urged others to conquer their reluctance too. Quite a service to the community I think.

Sometime we are reluctant to talk to God, to open up to him. Mobile phones can do all sorts of things. There is a whole world out there that is instantly accessible. But sometimes the person we really need to speak to is just simply there, waiting for us to talk. Ring any bells?

A reluctant pray-er prays

When I kept silent, my bones wasted away through my groaning all day long . . . Then I acknowledged my sin to you and did not cover up my iniquity.

Psalm 32: 3, 5

A prayer

Lord, there's been something I have been wanting to talk to you about. It's the way you found the time and opportunity to be alone with God. I am afraid many of us don't always do what is good or best for us, but you did things differently. Perhaps it was your prayer time that made you so un-reluctant when it came to speaking out against injustice. Un-reluctant when it came to taking up your cross too. Thanks for letting me just have a word. Amen

Stemming the tide

In 1991 I attended the East German Methodist Conference in Leipzig. One day a presentation was made – the World Methodist Peace Award – and it was given to an East German lady, Barbel Bohley, an artist who had been an advocate for peace and freedom. I got the impression that those at Conference might have chosen someone else if they had been given the choice, but when the presentation was made they all stood as one and applauded heartily, many with tears streaming down their faces. The wall had come down. They had won a freedom that just a short time before none of them could ever have imagined. It was just like a dream.

There are those special moments when we can scarcely believe what has happened and the enormity of it just hits us. From the relatively trivial experience of a lowly football team reaching a major final to matters of international importance. Psalm 126 remembers when God set the people of Israel free from their exile in Babylon. There was laughter and joyful exuberance. It was like dried river beds suddenly overflowing to the sound of running waters. It was just like an impossible dream come true. They remembered because they needed the tide of affairs to change once again.

Sometimes the course of events does not go the way people anticipate. You might expect 'if things go on as they are' that most of our chapels will close. But soon we shall be celebrating Easter. Maybe we shall find ourselves standing as one, with tears of laughter and delight because God in his unique way has broken through and conquered our cynicism and despair. And if that happens, what next?

It was like a dream

When the Lord restored the fortunes of Zion, we were like those who dreamed. Our mouths were filled with laughter, our tongues with songs of joy. Then it was said among the nations, 'The Lord has done great things for them.' The Lord has done great things for us, and we are filled with joy. Restore our fortunes, Lord, like streams in the Negev.

Psalm 126: 1–4

A prayer

Lord, do you remember that picture of King Canute, getting wet on the seashore as he vainly tried to stem the tide of the sea? You are a King who actually can stem tides – whether of despair, arrogance or complacency. Lord, do some great things among us. Do them today. Amen

Turning up the volume

What may be music to someone else's ears may not always be music to your own. When you enter what should be the peaceful sanctuary of your own home only to be faced with the jarring noise of someone else's musical peccadilloes, it can be somewhat taxing. The noise penetrates doors and windows and shreds fragile nerves. You cannot think properly; conversation becomes impossible. Finally you give in and shout upstairs: *Will you turn that down?*

Don't be deluded by the delicate wafting of palm branches as Jesus enters the city of Jerusalem. Or, for that matter, his seemingly innocuous entry into the city on a colt. Jesus is turning up the volume. Here is a king coming to claim his city. Here is Jesus on his way to overturning the tables (in more ways that one) in the Temple. The volume is getting higher. And while there are some who appear to like what they hear, there are also quite a few, especially the religious leaders, who would like him to turn the volume down.

When the perpetrators of that ungodly noise upstairs simply carry on regardless you may be tempted to issue threats. And they may well refuse to turn the volume down. But if there is a party going on up there, and they are not going to turn the volume down, then you may well have to consider your options. Welcome to Palm Sunday.

Palm Sunday

When he came near the place where the road goes down the Mount of Olives, the whole crowd of disciples began joyfully to praise God in loud voices for all the miracles they had seen:

'Blessed is the king who comes in the name of the Lord!'

'Peace in heaven and glory in the highest!'

Some of the Pharisees in the crowd said to Jesus, 'Teacher, rebuke your disciples!'

'I tell you,' he replied, 'if they keep quiet, the stones will cry out.'

Luke 19: 37–40

A prayer

Lord, if I have been too quiet about my faith, show me how I can turn up the volume. Amen

Don't forget the punchline

Some people are very good at telling jokes while other people couldn't tell one to save their lives. Then there are those who think they can tell jokes but when it comes to the punchline their memory either fails them completely or they get the punchline completely wrong.

Today is Easter Sunday. There is a punchline to the story which began in Bethlehem, which has taken us on a roller-coaster ride of love and faith, leading towards its denouement in Jerusalem and it is quite simple: *Christ is risen.* Don't forget it. Don't be embarrassed by it. Not today, not tomorrow.

There are some punchlines that leave you roaring in the aisles, some that leave you squirming in dismay, others that just leave you speechless. This is a punchline that grows on you. The punchline ought to have been: *Jesus died and that was the end of that!* After all they tried to hammer that home with devastating brutality. You just have to let the punchline ring for a while in your ears. Don't be surprised if a silence of incredulity gives way to wonder and then a rising swell of joy and excitement.

Christ is risen! It's a punchline that has a response. He is risen indeed. Alleluia!

Easter Sunday

On the first day of the week, very early in the morning, the women took the spices they had prepared and went to the tomb. They found the stone rolled away from the tomb, but when they entered, they did not find the body of the Lord Jesus. While they were wondering about this, suddenly two men in clothes that gleamed like lightning stood beside them. In their fright the women bowed down with their faces to the ground, but the men said to them, 'Why do you look for the living among the dead? He is not here; he has risen!'

Luke 24: 1–6a

A prayer

Lord, you remember that joke somebody told and I just didn't get it, and then the next day I did. Well this might be one of those days. Alleluia! Amen

The Cross for children

I recently had the privilege of being able to tell the Passion and Easter story to some very young children.

How much do your parents love you? I asked. I held my hands outstretched in front of me, six inches apart. That much? More, they said. My hands went further apart. That much? More, they said, and they were not satisfied till my hands were stretched out fully and I was standing in the shape of a cross.

What if you are naughty? I went on. Do they still love you, then? Oh yes, they said. My hands were again six inches apart. That much? But they were convinced that their parents' love was inexhaustible and once again my hands had to be widened as far apart as they could go.

I told the children that when Jesus died he wanted to show people God would always love them, too. [I kept the shape of the cross.] That much! Jesus died on a cross like that, I said, with his arms stretched out. Not very nice, but Jesus believed that God loved people when they were good, when they were naughty and even when they were very very bad. It really hurt Jesus on the cross, you know; it was very hard, and eventually he died, but just like his Father God he never stopped loving – he even kept on loving the people who were hurting him so much. That's amazing, isn't it?

Easter Sunday

These [things] are written so that you may come to believe that Jesus is the Messiah, the Son of God, and that through believing you may have life in his name.

John 20: 19

A prayer

Lord, I can't imagine what it would be like to be crucified. How did you manage to go on loving people when you were in so much pain, and even the very ones who had caused it all? It might have made perfect sense to children, but me? I am just speechless. You take a simple bit of faith – God is love – and you push it as far as it will go. And then some. You, Lord, are very disturbing. Amen

Hearing about Easter for the first time

Sometimes we make life and faith a little too complicated. One of the great joys of talking to and with children is that you have to get to the heart of things and make things simple.

I was writing last week about speaking to some very young children. After talking about the crucifixion we got on to the Resurrection. I told them: When it was all over, Jesus was buried in a garden. A big round stone was rolled in front of the hole into the place where he was buried, and it was impossible to get in or out. Then everyone went home to sleep. And the next night they slept too. But the next morning, when they went to the garden you know that stone had been rolled away and Jesus wasn't there any more. You'd never guess, but God had brought him back to life again.

I will never forget the look of amazement and delight on the face of one young boy. He had heard the story we are so familiar with for the first time. He had not known the ending. And I was reminded of the extraordinary power of the Easter Gospel. I am sure some people believe because they are very childlike and will believe anything; I am sure we might think some people believe because they are gullible. But people can also believe because they know the truth when they hear it.

Don't underestimate the degree to which children may get to know God.

Now it was Mary Magdalene and Joanna and Mary the mother of James and the other women with them who told these things to the apostles, but these words seemed to them an idle tale, and they did not believe them. But Peter rose and ran to the tomb; stooping and looking in, he saw the linen cloths by themselves; and he went home marvelling at what had happened.

Luke 24: 10–12

A prayer

Lord, you know there is something a little bit embarrassing about the Resurrection. I mean it's so incredible, isn't it? Do you ever wonder why so many just dismiss it out of hand? Could you have thought of something, well, a little less divine? For anyone to believe that, well you would have to experience something, too, wouldn't you? Amen

A ghostly apparition?

I don't know whether you go in for ghost stories, but in Jesus' day they certainly did. I am sure the average life-expectancy then was quite low, but of course many did reach their three score years and ten. If by chance your life was cut short by ill health, violence or because you had had an accident, people believed that your ghost might live on in a kind of underworld – especially if you hadn't been buried properly. It sounds a bit spooky. Really, it's how people expressed a sense that death had conquered them, taken them too soon.

A couple of days after Jesus died, and he would have been in his early 30s, some rumours started circulating that Jesus had been seen. Questions would have surfaced as to whether he had been buried properly. And when the disciples saw the risen Jesus, their first thought was that they were seeing his ghost. That explains why they were so frightened. Jesus had died and his mission had failed. And they had failed him too.

But death had not conquered Jesus. He asked his disciples to touch him, and eat with him. He was not standing there to haunt them or remind them of their failures. Jesus was there as a sign of new life and hope. His mission in a sense was just beginning and he wanted them to be a part of it. You and me, too.

While they were still talking about this, Jesus himself stood among them and said to them, 'Peace be with you.' They were startled and frightened, thinking they saw a ghost. He said to them, 'Why are you troubled, and why do doubts rise in your minds? Look at my hands and my feet. It is I myself! Touch me and see; a ghost does not have flesh and bones, as you see I have.' When he had said this, he showed them his hands and feet. And while they still did not believe it because of joy and amazement, he asked them, 'Do you have anything here to eat?' They gave him a piece of broiled fish, and he took it and ate it in their presence.

Luke 24: 36–43

A prayer

Lord, it's good to know that you don't haunt us or condemn us for our failures either. I suspect you just want us to believe that the incredible has happened and you are with us. Lord, I believe. Help me when my faith falls short. Amen

Simeon's Mum

As I write this letter a new Pope has just been elected. At his installation, the Cardinals (all men) gathered in seeming droves, and only one woman took part in the service. This is nothing new.

Back in the year 63, James, the brother of Jesus, and the first Bishop of Jerusalem, was killed at the instigation of the high priest. By common consent a new Bishop was named; his name was Simeon. Now Simeon was the son of Cleopas who happened to have been one of the two disciples that the risen Lord had met on the way to Emmaus. The question is: who was the other one? This other disciple is not named, and perhaps the most likely explanation for that is because she was a woman. [Women tend to get named even in the New Testament only when no men are present!] A woman would not be expected to speak to another man in public. Jesus also gets invited into *their* home. The other disciple, in all probability, is Cleopas' wife.

Now Cleopas' wife is named in John's Gospel and her name is Mary. She was probably more significant than you might think. She was one of those who stood at the Cross, and possibly had first-hand experience of being at the empty tomb. It's not just those who are specially named who are necessarily the most significant people. I would like to think that Simeon mentioned his Mum when he was elected.

The Easter testimony of unnamed women

In addition, some of our women amazed us. They went to the tomb early this morning but didn't find his body. They came and told us that they had seen a vision of angels, who said he was alive.

Luke 24: 22–23

A prayer

Lord, today I want to pray for Pope Francis. He seems like a breath of fresh air. And Lord, I also want to thank you for the loyal and faithful devotion of so many women in our congregations. Forgive us when we have not recognized the people we ought to have. To such you appeared as risen Lord. From Simeon to Francis, we have a legacy to be very thankful for. Amen

Thomas, Christian first class

One of the things I have never understood is why people leave football matches a few minutes before they finish. Yes, I know they avoid the traffic and get home quicker, but how many times have they missed the most decisive action in the game? Football is littered with last-minute goals, and I wouldn't want to miss them!

You have to feel sorry for Thomas. The risen Jesus appeared to the other disciples while he was out. Talk about bad timing. Thomas missed the Resurrection. But as a result of this his experience added something to the quality of the story. Thomas did not take the joy and excitement of the other disciples as overwhelming evidence. He felt that he would have to be able to see Jesus himself – and even put his hands in his side. He had to wait another week before he saw the risen Lord.

'Doubting Thomas', as he has unfairly been called, is at least an honest doubter. He demands that we don't live off the experiences of other people. He looks for alternative explanations other than the ones he has been given. He doesn't just go along with the 'party line' without thinking things through. He is confused and uncertain but he demands honesty and integrity through it all.

And at the end of the day, his experience of the risen Lord, is every bit as valid and important as that of the other disciples. Ordinary he might be, maybe even unremarkable and stubborn, but he is not a second-class Christian. He may have missed the Resurrection but the risen Lord has not missed him.

Easter Sunday

A week later his [Jesus'] disciples were in the house again, and Thomas was with them. Though the doors were locked, Jesus came and stood among them and said, 'Peace be with you!' Then he said to Thomas, 'Put your finger here; see my hands. Reach out your hand and put it into my side. Stop doubting and believe.'

Thomas said to him, 'My Lord and my God!'

John 20: 26–28

A prayer

Lord, thank you for those times when you get me to the right place at the right time. Sometimes, though, I just miss them. When that happens I pray that you will just work in my life so that, even a week later – or even longer – your will may be done. Amen

Pentecost at Mow Cop

One of the great Old Testament stories is about Naaman, a high-ranking Syrian soldier who contracts leprosy. The message from the prophet Elisha is that he should take a dip seven times in the River Jordan. Naaman is not best pleased. He suspects he is being fobbed off and why on earth should he go to the Jordan when the rivers nearby are clearly superior.

Without any pretensions to being a prophet, I would like to ask you to come to Mow Cop next Sunday at 3.00 am for the Camp Meeting. It should be a really good Circuit occasion. You can probably think of all kinds of reasons (Naaman-like) why you shouldn't: *It's bound to be cold. It's too remote. I don't do outdoors. They won't sing the hymns I like. Surely it would be better somewhere else. I don't do Camp. It's all rather pointless. I leave that sort of thing to the younger ones. I only worship at my own church. I can think of better things to do. And even if I can't . . .*

It's not hard to think of excuses. You could come up with dozens. But this is Pentecost we are talking about and a celebration of the gift of the Spirit. God has a habit of doing what he does best in (seemingly) unlikely places. So why not put aside the excuses this time? Bring a chair or a blanket. Enjoy God in the open air. There are some things worth doing for no other reason than to glorify God.

As for Naaman, he went to the River Jordan and was cured. I could have asked you to take a dip in the River Dane. Personally, I'd prefer Mow Cop.

Naaman's story

But Naaman went away angry and said . . . 'Are not Abana and Pharpar, the rivers of Damascus, better than all the waters of Israel? Couldn't I wash in them and be cleansed?' So he turned and went off in a rage. Naaman's servants went to him and said, 'My father, if the prophet had told you to do some great thing, would you not have done it? How much more, then, when he tells you, "Wash and be cleansed"!' So he went down and dipped himself in the Jordan seven times, as the man of God had told him, and his flesh was restored and became clean like that of a young boy.

2 Kings 5: 11–14

A prayer

Lord, forgive me when I 'pull rank'. Forgive me when I think my wisdom is higher than yours. Forgive me when I look down upon 'other places'. Forgive me when I get angry. Forgive me when I constrain your Spirit. I don't suppose you are finished with healing yet, are you Lord? Amen

Spreading the fire

I don't suppose there will be many of you – but certainly some – that have ever designed a building, or a tunnel, a ship or even a submarine. But if you did you would need to take account of the dangers posed by a fire. You might need to design things in such a way that if a fire broke out, it could be contained in particular compartments. By doing that you could save people's lives and possibly the building, the tunnel or the ship. I am told this is called passive fire protection.

Tongues of flame were reported when the first disciples received the Spirit on the day of Pentecost. It all sounds rather alarming, but don't worry, we Christians are actually very good at passive fire protection. We divide our lives into compartments: home, family, work, holidays, money, church, garden, interests, friends, politics, sex and shopping. If the fire of God's Spirit should threaten any of these compartments they can be conveniently sealed off. That's a relief then!

Well it might have been if today wasn't Pentecost. Because this is the day when God challenges us firstly to look at those areas in our lives to which we have conveniently said (to him): *No admittance.* And then – and this may not be easy – to imagine what our lives would be like if we opened up those areas to the Spirit.

This is called active fire spreading. It is usually accompanied by new beginnings, re-designed lives and changed priorities. Pentecost without fire is never going to set us alight.

The Day of Pentecost

When the day of Pentecost came, all the believers were gathered together in one place. Suddenly there was a noise from the sky which sounded like a strong wind blowing, and it filled the whole house where they were sitting. Then they saw what looked like tongues of fire which spread out and touched each person there.

Acts 2: 1–3

A prayer

Lord, the warmth of a good log fire or the soft ambience of a room full of candles is all very alluring and welcoming, but I suspect your kind of fire goes much deeper. That's why I am safe in my protected area where you can't get through. I'll come out and have a chat with you later, when it's safer. You don't mind doing things on my terms do you? Lord . . . you are not supposed to be in here! Amen

Hillsborough and truth

In 2012 the Hillsborough Independent Panel published their report on the Hillsborough disaster. It found that fans were not to blame for the crush that killed 96 people in 1989. It led to the original verdict being quashed and new inquests ordered. Just recently Anne Williams, one of the campaigners for truth and justice, received an emotional farewell at her funeral. As the cortège disappeared the crowd burst into spontaneous applause.

Her campaign, I suppose, was based on the premise that there are some truths to which we all have a right. People used to make play on the notion that the first casualty of war is truth. Lies, propaganda, misinformation and cover-ups soon follow. But clearly they are not the province of war alone. Getting to the truth of something then was no easier in Jesus' day than in our own. Secrecy, lying and deception were alive and well then, too. Telling lies could even be considered an honourable thing to do – if you thought someone was not entitled to the truth.

When Jesus mentioned the Spirit he sometimes spoke of the *Spirit of truth.* There are, indeed, some truths to which we all have a right. And one of the things the Spirit does is lead us to the truth – about God, about Jesus, about ourselves. God clearly thinks you and I have a right to that. We live in an age when most people do not hold belief in God in particularly high esteem. We may sometimes even wonder whether they are right. *Truly, truly, I say to you* was one of Jesus's ways of assuring people he was telling the truth. The Spirit assures us today of much the same. It may take a long time, but that truth will come out in the end.

Easter Sunday

When, however, the Spirit comes, who reveals the truth about God, he will lead you into all the truth. He will not speak on his own authority, but he will speak of what he hears and will tell you of things to come.

John 16: 13

A prayer

Lord, Let me just thank you for holding on to the truth when it would have been so easy to let go. I don't suppose you even had the comfort of spontaneous applause when you were buried. As we worship you and try to serve you, we trust you to fill us with your Spirit so that we, too, are not ashamed to tell the truth about you and your love, and indeed to hold on to it. Amen

My way

I suppose one of the most famous of songs is *My Way*. It was written by Paul Anka for Frank Sinatra. It tells the story of a man who has grown old, and looks back on his life as death approaches. He is comfortable with his mortality and he takes responsibility for how he has dealt with all the challenges life has thrown at him. I tend to hear it mostly at funerals nowadays, which is not surprising. It celebrates someone's uniqueness, distinctiveness and independence.

There is a place for that. Strangely enough though, in Jesus' day people were not valued because they were unique but because of their link with something or someone else. It could be the place they came from (Simon of Cyrene, Paul of Tarsus), the nation they belonged to (Israelites), or their clan (Mary was 'of the house of David'). It could mean their family ties: James and John were referred to as the sons of Zebedee. It may smack of stereotyping, but then people wanted to know about those other links because that might give them an idea of *the way* you would do things. They would assume those other ties would have shaped your life.

We may (quite rightly) value our distinctiveness and what makes us unique. We may take pride in doing things 'our way'. *I ate it up and I spit it out*, the song goes. We may or may not care a hoot what anyone else says about the way we do things. But part of Christian humility (and love) is to allow ourselves to be shaped by one another, too – and pre-eminently by Jesus. So that, in the challenges life throws at us, we also do things his way and sing about it.

For we are all partners with Christ if we hold firmly to the end the confidence we had at the beginning. This is what the scripture says: 'If you hear God's voice today, do not be stubborn, as your ancestors were when they rebelled against God.'

Hebrews 3: 15–16

A prayer

Lord, I have this dream where I am trying to tell you as humbly as I possibly can that my way is usually, if not invariably, the right way. Someone is playing Frank Sinatra in the background. And all you do, Lord, is just ignore me and keep introducing me to Brother So-and-So and Sister So-and-So. Can you please explain yourself, Lord? Amen

The curiosity that cures the cat

Curiosity killed the cat, you know. And yes, curiosity does have its downsides. Pandora opened the box of suffering, unleashing untold misery. Prometheus stole fire from the gods and got punished for it. Eve wanted to know what the forbidden fruit tasted like. What happened to the proverbial cat, I can't exactly tell you.

And yet curiosity can be good. The National Trust Magazine arrived today inviting me to come and see how people lived in days gone by. There is an almost insatiable appetite for finding out more about people's lives, discovering new information, new knowledge. The world has advanced in many ways simply because people have been curious and wanted to marvel and ask simple questions like: how? and why?

Curiosity in Jesus' day was not regarded very positively. It might tempt you away from accepting things as they have always been. And you wouldn't want people searching for skeletons in the cupboard, would you? On the other hand people were very curious about Jesus. They followed him into the desert and came in their thousands to hear what he had to say and see what he might do next.

Curiosity is related to the Middle English word *cure*, which has to do with care and attention. It is related to words like curate (one who has cure of souls), curator and accurate. Curiosity's heritage is linked with healing not harming. Why is it then that when we come to church we are not particularly curious as to what each other believes and why? Curiosity might even sometimes cure the cat.

Paul assumes other Christians will be curious about him

Tychicus, our dear brother and faithful servant in the Lord's work, will give you all the news about me, so that you may know how I am getting along. That is why I am sending him to you – to tell you how all of us are getting along and to encourage you.

Ephesians 6: 1–3

A prayer

Lord, you know how private we can be when it comes to our faith. Getting the balance right between care and attention, giving people the curiosity and interest they deserve and not being too intrusive does not come easy you know! Lord, neither let my curiosity hinder me from encouraging others; not let my lack of it lead to discouraging others. Amen

When Jeremy rang

Today Jeremy rang. I don't think it was his real name. The accent seemed more Mumbai than Macclesfield and he was trying to sell me something I didn't want. Not only that, I was busy searching for my car keys and waiting for a really important call. What this required now was considerable patience. Patience is something we feel we need when we are going at a different pace than we would really like to be going. Sometimes we feel slowed down and stuck in the traffic. At other times things are changing faster than we can keep up with. It all takes patience.

And patience is one of the fruits of the Spirit. However, what you and I think of as patience and what the Bible thinks of as patience may not be quite the same thing. In Mediterranean culture patience was a gift you needed when things were not likely to change very much at all, when things just stayed as they were – or got worse. You might be ill, lose your status, your family and friends. The question then was whether, under those circumstances, you would continue to trust God and be faithful to him, or whether you would turn away and rebel against him.

Jesus once pointed to a woman who exemplified that kind of patience, a widow who for all her poverty and, presumably, bellyful of anxieties was determined to live with compassion and generosity. Patience of a different order indeed.

New Testament patience

As Jesus sat near the Temple treasury, he watched the people as they dropped in their money. Many rich men dropped in a lot of money; then a poor widow came along and dropped in two little copper coins, worth about a penny. He called his disciples together and said to them, 'I tell you that this poor widow put more in the offering box than all the others. For the others put in what they had to spare of their riches; but she, poor as she is, put in all she had – she gave all she had to live on.'

Mark 12: 41–44

A prayer

Lord, sometimes we don't change much, do we? We continue in our own sweet way, regardless of the promises we keep making. And you patiently continue to love us and be generous towards us. That widow you noticed puts me to shame. She still trusted you, giving when she had nothing. Lord, give me that kind of patience. Amen

Earl Grey and Victoria sponge

When I lived in the Middle East I was occasionally invited out to someone's home. Complimentary remarks I may have made about the orange trees resulted in gifts of oranges; 'A nice table' or 'What a splendid picture' rebounded with 'It is yours. Everything I have is yours.' (Not to be taken too literally.) I was very careful what I said about my hosts' daughter.

The rules of hospitality vary in different cultures. We tend to invite our friends round for a meal. They may stay overnight but when it comes to strangers we might prefer to recommend a suitable hotel. Those asking for money may be directed to Social Services. At the time of Jesus, hospitality was something you offered primarily to strangers. You would want to know who the stranger was, whether he presented a threat to your village, and whether he would conform to local customs. So, over the meal table, the guest would be tested with questions and might be invited to speak. At the end of the meal the guest would leave either as a friend or as an enemy. Host and guest may well now have mutual obligations to one another.

One of the famous Gospel incidents was when Jesus invited himself round to the house of the tax-collector Zacchaeus for tea – somewhat breaking the cultural mould. I suspect Jesus was not just honouring Zacchaeus. Nor would he make just polite conversation about the oranges and Zacchaeus' home decor. I suspect, in a classic bit of role reversal, he would be testing out Zacchaeus and his newly declared intentions. If we have invited Jesus into our lives we should not expect any less.

Jesus testing out his host Simon over dinner

'There were two men who owed money to a moneylender,' Jesus began. 'One owed him five hundred silver coins, and the other owed him fifty. Neither of them could pay him back, so he cancelled the debts of both. Which one, then, will love him more?'

Luke 7: 41–42

A prayer

Lord, I suspect that if you came to my house for tea you would be less interested in a cup of Earl Grey and a Victoria sponge cake than in what kind of disciple I am. I imagine an evening of much hilarity punctuated by some very searching questions. Is heaven a bit like that? Amen

Living the dream

I went into prison one morning and asked an officer how he was. *Oh, I am living the dream,* he said, rather caustically. I was left in no doubt that he was living anything but! We have been brought up to expect that economies and incomes will expand every year, that there will be unlimited reserves of minerals, power and dreams. And that we ought to have a part of it. *There is always more where that came from,* the saying goes.

In some parts of the world – and that includes the Mediterranean area at the time of Jesus – people don't actually think like that. The perception would be that the good things of life – beauty, health, wealth, land and reputation – only exist in a limited (and usually short) supply. They might say: *there is no more where that came from.* Rich people were often the object of suspicion because what they had must have been taken from somebody else!

The disciples of John the Baptist were once worried that their master's fame was being overtaken by that of Jesus. They were right; it was. But, as it happened, John was not envious and simply said: *He must increase, and I must decrease.* Reputation was a limited commodity so that's how it worked. The authorities also regarded Jesus' growing reputation as diminishing theirs – but they were not as gracious as John. They were determined to put a stop to it.

Jesus never promised people they would all be able to live the dream but he did say that, contrary to the general outlook, he could offer some things that would never run out. I think John the Baptist understood that.

Jesus speaking to the Samaritan woman at the well

'Those who drink this water will get thirsty again, but those who drink the water that I will give them will never be thirsty again. The water that I will give them will become in them a spring which will provide them with life-giving water and give them eternal life.'

John 4: 13–14

A prayer

Lord, I have to say I am pretty impressed with John the Baptist. When the things you really want are in short supply, to have that kind of grace and that lack of envy is remarkable. Lord, show me the way to the well. Amen

How am I supposed to live off that?

The young woman looked up at me, reproachfully. I don't think much of churches. They don't feed you very well. All I got when I went was a little piece of bread. How am I supposed to live off that? I had to explain that if she was hungry she would be better off going to one of our pea and pie suppers. But to understand the particular meal she went to you had to be hungry for something else.

Often we come together to eat when we have a special celebration that affects us all. It might be the Christmas lunch or the Harvest Supper. Everyone is invited and the meal celebrates the fact that we belong to one another and to Christ.

On other occasions we are invited to a special celebration in someone else's life. It might be a wedding or a special anniversary. It might be sharing a piece of cake after a baptism, or a farewell dinner when someone goes off to university or moves house. These meals often mark the transitional moments in someone's life (or the celebration of an earlier one) when a fundamental change takes place.

When Jesus met with his disciples for their final meal, those two scenarios came together. They were sharing in the annual and traditional celebration of Passover. But it was to become a special occasion for Jesus. This was going to be his last meal with his disciples. He was going to die the next day. This meal was a transitional moment for all of them.

He placed a little piece of bread into each of their hands – and we have been living off that moment for years.

Jesus breaks bread

. . . the Lord Jesus on the night when he was betrayed took a loaf of bread, and when he had given thanks he broke it and said: 'This is my body given for you.'

1 Corinthians 11: 23–24

A prayer

Lord, you do get those days, don't you? Sometimes you expect them and sometimes they just turn up. Those days, happy or sad, frightening or exciting, when something changes and life is never the same. Sometimes I wonder how we will manage, but there always seems to be plenty of bread left at your table. Amen

Thank you and goodbye

On Father's Day, one of my children rang me up to wish me a good day. Then he asked for some money. You may well be familiar with the picture. I did not mind but when he got the money he forgot to say 'thank you'. Irksome or what? I have since discovered that in certain cultures it might actually be insulting to say 'thank you'. In parts of India if you said 'thank you' to a close friend or family member when they had given you a lift in their car it would seem like they weren't important to you anymore – just a taxi driver. No need to say thanks. That's what family and friends do. In China you are supposed to be modest, so when someone compliments you on your stunning hat you tell them it's naff. If you say 'thank you', it's rude.

You know there is only one occasion in the New Testament where anyone ever said 'thank you' to Jesus. It was the leper – one of 10 who were healed – who came to Jesus. Back then if you said 'thank you' it meant *Thanks and goodbye. That's the end of our relationship.* That leper was a Samaritan and he presumably thought that would be the last he would see of Jesus, him being a Jew and all that.

It didn't mean you weren't grateful if you didn't say 'thank you'. I don't suppose Jesus was bothered that the other 9 lepers didn't say 'thank you' to him. It did bother him that they didn't praise God for what had happened. If you were really grateful then to someone you sang their praises. Especially in situations when they have done something for you you could never do for them. There are times when 'thank you' doesn't seem enough anyway. I hope my son does not read this. He would probably tell me he just hadn't wanted to cause any offence and end our relationship.

Jesus speaking to the Samaritan and former leper

One of them, when he saw he was healed, came back, praising God in a loud voice. He threw himself at Jesus' feet and thanked him – and he was a Samaritan. Jesus asked, 'Were not all ten cleansed? Where are the other nine? Has no one returned to give praise to God except this foreigner?'

Luke 17: 15–18

A prayer

Lord, forgive me when I have exchanged real gratitude for a couple of cheap words. You have done things that I could never do. You died for me. You forgave my sins. Far from ending relationships you have sought to renew them and restore them. Would you accept now the thanks of a grateful heart? Amen

I forgot the attachment

Oh, they are very attached you know. Well you could be talking about two friends, a lady and her dog, a man and his wallet or a child and his blanket. Attachments are very important, and what we are attached to tells us a lot about the kind of people we are. We are attached to the people we love.

Of course not all attachments are healthy. We may be more attached to places than people (or God). Not all attachments are permanent. I have noticed many people in prison forming very close bonds and relationships. They rarely last the course once outside the prison walls. And not all attachments are loving. You can be closely involved in one group or another, then when you decide that group no longer meets your personal interests you can up sticks and move on.

Don't let that diminish the startling truth that God is profoundly attached to us. As John puts it: God so loved (i.e. was so attached) to the world he gave his only son. This is no mild flirtation, or an attachment that will not last the test of time. This is God saying he is so attached to us that he has done something about it and indeed pushed his love to the limits.

All of which begs the question about our attachment to God. Sometimes people send (or try to send) an email with an attachment; that is to say, a letter, photo or some other document. Only they forget the attachment and it is not there. It's easily done. We can talk about loving God till we are blue in the face but if our attachment has gone missing then we need to do something about it.

From the Old Testament

But be very careful to keep the commandment and the law that Moses the servant of the Lord gave you: to love the Lord your God, to walk in obedience to him, to keep his commands, to hold fast to him and to serve him with all your heart and with all your soul.

Joshua 22: 5

A prayer

Lord, you may not have noticed, but I am very attached to my creature comforts, my home, my family, my computer, my books. I hope you are still up for forgiveness when I have not been quite so attached to you. I was just wondering whether, when it comes to serving you with all my heart and all my soul, we could just modify the *all* bit? Just asking. Amen

Him serve with mirth

I have a little bee in my bonnet. I don't like hymns being sung too slow. *All people that on earth do dwell* (STF 1) should be a lively hymn, but it's often sung at a funereal pace. By the time you have got to *Him serve with mirth, his praise forth tell* the capacity for mirth has been profoundly diminished. And that is only the third line!

The thing is that *mirth* is indeed something with which we should serve God. Not, that you would always believe it, as you look across some congregations. It may not be a common word now but it carries with it a number of connotations – laughter, humour, ridicule, irony, exuberance, even smiles. When you read the Bible sometimes you have to think how Jesus said things; you have to imagine the twinkle in his eye and the laughter in his voice.

People would have laughed at the sheer absurdity of placing a lamp under a bushel or the image of a man with a plank in his eye. John the Baptist spoke of Pharisees and Sadducees as if they were snakes fleeing from a forest fire. And Jesus came up with some pearlers. I think my favourite is *You strain out a gnat but swallow a camel.* The Pharisees were indeed usually the butt of his jokes too.

We know that laughter lightens the mood, relieves a tense moment, pricks the bubble of the pompous, gives people courage and can even help us look at things we might normally ignore – especially about ourselves. It also brings us together. Yes it can be cruel and malicious too. But rightly used, *mirth* is a wonderful way of serving God. Enjoy it. I just wish we could get to it a bit quicker.

Then our mouth was filled with laughter, and our tongue with shouts of joy; then they said among the nations, 'The Lord has done great things for them.'

Psalm 126: 2

A prayer

Lord, thank you for those whose sense of humour, vitality and life lifts us up, brings us together and strengthens us. May the joy you came to bring be evident in our voices and faces. Amen

Green with envy

What's the meaning of the green shirt then, Philip?, asked the prison officer perhaps wondering if my new clerical shirt denoted a promotion to some special office. Wimbledon Chaplain, I replied, almost with a touch of conviction. Oh, I see, he said. Sadly a raise of his eyebrows indicated he believed not one word of it. Actually a number of people have asked about the significance of my shirt, so I have decided to invest it with some: it's there to absorb envy. Sounds odd? Well, there are still plenty who are green with it.

And Christians are no less susceptible to envy than anyone else. Some look at the 'success' of other churches, and think 'if only we had their Minister, their children, their money, we could do great things too!' Some cringe when someone else is recognized or applauded, thinking to themselves 'well my hotpot was just as good'. Others simply wish they were as gifted as others. The problem with envy is that it is destructive. The effects can be long lasting.

Jesus was once approached by a woman with a chronic gynaecological complaint. She made for Jesus and touched the hem of his garment [Luke 8: 44]. What she would have touched were the tassels of Jesus' cloak and these tassels were believed to protect you from envy. It makes you wonder if, on top of her obvious complaint, this woman was envious of everyone else who seemed to have everything going for them. The remarkable thing was, when she touched Jesus she was healed. Maybe of her envy, too.

How do you absorb envy? Enjoy one another. Be happy in their gifts. Be glad when good things happen to them. That applies to other churches too! It can be very healing. And if the shirt fits, wear it.

Pilate said to them [the crowd], 'Whom do you want me to release for you, Barabbas or Jesus who is called Christ?' For he knew that it was out of envy that they had delivered him up.

Matthew 27: 17–18

A prayer

Lord, forgive me when I am envious of the successes and the lives of others. Forgive me when I am envious of the things they can do that I can't. Forgive me when I am envious because they can simply do things better. Lord, I come to touch the hem of your garment. Heal me, too. Amen

Town centre priorities

When I go into the town centre I often witness a strange but not unusual spectacle. Two or three people bump into one another. They don't just say hello. They stop and talk. And when I have been to the post office and the bank or had my haircut, they are still there engrossed in conversation. It would probably be a mistake to think they are any the less busy than anyone else. They just realise that greeting people takes time.

It is easy to reduce greeting people to a quick hello and how-do-you-do. In Jesus' day, greeting people always took time, sometimes hours. You had a drink together, you debated, argued, passed on bits of news, gossiped and maybe did some business. Greetings – the real ones – are not just about exchanging pleasantries. They are the means by which we establish relationships.

I wonder how it would sound if every now and again preachers (or Ministers) brought the greetings of their church with them when they came to take a service elsewhere. It might be just a short letter sharing some news or cause for concern or celebration, or a request for prayer. Just read the beginnings and endings of Paul's letters. Greetings strengthen people.

It may be that we are too busy doing other things, which in the immediacy of the moment seems much more important. Thankfully, there are always people chatting in the town centre to remind us of a different set of priorities.

Greet all God's people in Christ Jesus. The brothers and sisters who are with me send greetings. All God's people here send you greetings, especially those who belong to Caesar's household. The grace of the Lord Jesus Christ be with your spirit. Amen

Philippians 4: 21–23

A prayer

Lord, we are busy people you know. It's not just things at church that take time. I have a life elsewhere you know. Paul was very generous with his 'alls'. Was he exaggerating? I think so. Amen.

P.S. By the way, it was good to hear that John had been praying for me. That really helped. Amen

The first line of trust

My car is in the first line of trust. I look after it, feed it with petrol, oil and water, and service it once a year. I trust it every day. I know that tomorrow it will get me to where I want to go and on time. If I am late, I know it won't be the car's fault. It will be because I have got stuck in traffic (possible) or have lost the keys (more likely). I trust my car implicitly.

Not that my trust is absolutely boundless. Not at all. It is conceivable that the car might break down and I won't be able to repair it myself. Or, I might hit some black ice and skid off the road. Someone might even run into the back of me. However I do have a second line of trust. I belong to the RAC and I can trust them, too. They will come along, mend the car, or at least get it safely to a garage and me home.

However, it is equally conceivable that this could happen on the busiest bank holiday of the year when everyone else wants the RAC, and when half of their men (or women) have been struck down with flu. *We will be there, sir, but it may take several hours.* I may not be able to wait that long. So I turn to my third line of trust – the family. Surely there will be one of them who will be able to down tools and come and pick me up?

We often say we trust God. He'll get us there. He'll listen to us when we need him. My guess is that in practice when it comes to trusting God it's some way down the line. For Jesus, the God he knew as Father was the first line of trust.

On the cross they mocked Jesus

He trusts in God. Let God rescue him now if he wants him, for he said, 'I am the Son of God.' In the same way the rebels who were crucified with him also heaped insults on him.

Matthew 27: 43–44

A prayer

Lord, they were right, though, weren't they? For all their jibes and insults those leaders threw at you, you did trust in God. You didn't wait till you were desperate. You trusted him all along. Even when things were unbelievably painful you trusted him. Amen

School's over

I remember the incident well. We were playing football. It was a good game and then a penalty was awarded. Immediately a dispute ensued but not the one you might expect. The argument was not between the opposing sides, but between the two lads who wanted to take the penalty. One argued (quite convincingly for the majority) that he was the best penalty-taker. The other said it was his ball, promptly picked it up and walked off. Game abandoned.

The politics of the schoolyard should not be part of our life as Christians. When you, or anybody else, give a ball or some money to the church it ceases to be yours. Who does it belong to now? We can maintain the illusion that it is still ours. I once came across the ludicrous situation of a man who donated a brick to the church years ago, fell out with someone and now wanted it back! I confess I was tempted to give it him. But the money (or brick) has now become a gift. It does not belong to you any more. It does not even belong to your church. Nor does it belong to the Circuit. It belongs to God. We simply act as trustees, and it is our responsibility to use the gifts we have given and been given responsibly and for what we determine together as the real work of God. Otherwise, game over.

But still it persists. *It's our money really. We can spend it on what we like. We gave it. Morally it is ours.* But that is the boy with the ball talking. Christian maturity comes into play when we can truly stand back from our own self-interests and ask the question: *Now what would God want us to spend this money on?* Game on.

All the believers were one in heart and mind. No one claimed that any of their possessions was their own, but they shared everything they had. With great power the apostles continued to testify to the resurrection of the Lord Jesus. And God's grace was so powerfully at work in them all that there was no needy person among them. For from time to time those who owned land or houses sold them, brought the money from the sales and put it at the apostles' feet, and it was distributed to anyone who had need.

Acts 4: 33–35

A prayer

Lord, when I say that everything I have is *yours*, I am of course assuming that this is just a turn of phrase and that in practice I can still treat it as mine? You can't surely mean there are no strings attached. Not even little ones? Lord, it's not as easy to let go as I thought. Amen

Crossed wires

It can be a bit embarrassing can't it? There you are talking on the phone to Great Aunt Matilda trying to reassure her that her new hat really is the height of fashion. Are you sure? *Of course . . .* At which point your sister appears in the doorway in her new outfit. Tara! Your attention is diverted and instinctively you say *I wouldn't be seen dead in that.* Great Aunt Matilda immediately dissolves into floods of tears. *No, no, I wasn't talking to you.*

With Jesus, it's the other way round. We read the stories about him and the parables he told. We think he is talking to them, to the rich young man, or the Pharisees, or the disciples and we kind of listen in. We think, how stupid can those disciples get? Or, that'll bring those Pharisees down a peg or two. And then the penny drops. He is not just talking to them. It's as if a voice suddenly declares: *No, no, I was talking to you.* A bit embarrassing, really.

Some people need as much convincing that God is talking to them, as Aunt Matilda needed that you weren't speaking to her. But that's the way the Bible works. Jesus speaks to 'them' and to you at the same time.

There was once a man who went away to study for a number of years. When he came back home his father asked him what he had learned. He said: I have learned that you should love your neighbour as yourself. The father was perplexed: It took you all those years to work that out? I thought you knew that before. Yes, the son replied, but now I know what it means that *I* should love my neighbour as myself.

Love the Lord your God with all your heart and with all your soul and with all your strength.

Deuteronomy 6: 5

A prayer

Lord, I am comfortable with you wanting others to love you with all of their heart, their soul and their strength. I thought you were prepared to make an exception in my case. Clearly not. Are you sure you weren't talking to someone else? Amen

When you are at your worst

You know the sort. She has the voice and appearance of an angel. Butter would not melt in her mouth. She moves along unruffled by the minor irritations that would upset lesser mortals. But press a different set of buttons and just see how her demeanour changes. And the language? Well it's an education!

The Psalms show us faith, hurt, joy, anger, doubt, strength, vulnerability, maybe all in the same person. *The Lord is gracious and merciful, slow to anger and abounding in steadfast love. The Lord is good to all . . .* [Psalm 145]. Well you couldn't imagine him getting cross, could you? Mind you, you should listen to Psalm 89: *How long, O Lord, will you hide yourself for ever? How long will your wrath burn like fire? Remember how short my time is . . .* He is about to explode! Maybe this is two different people. More likely, it is the same person on two very different days.

The Psalms can be as abrasive as some people's language. They bring you face to face with God not only when you have got your best face on, but also when you are pretty raw. Jesus chipped away at people's pretensions, too. He levelled a charge of hypocrisy on some really rather good people, when they were pretending to be something they weren't. It wasn't about one-upmanship. It's simply that if you want to know a new kind of joy in your life then you have to abandon the pretence, the illusion that you have got it all together all the time. If you truly believe God is a God of love then accept that he loves you when you are at your worst. Then maybe he can do his stuff.

[P.S. The character above is entirely fictitious. All attempts to identify the person in mind will be fruitless!]

Having learned things the hard way I finally worked it out . . .

The Lord is gracious and merciful, slow to anger and abounding in steadfast love. The Lord is good to all.

Psalm 145: 8

A prayer

Lord, I know you came so that we might have life in all its fulness and all that, but can't I just stick to the Psalms that make me feel good? I have that lurking fear that if I come to you as I really am, you might not like what you see. But then I suppose that's not where your love stops, is it? Amen

The Umbrella Project

We were stopped by airport security. The x-ray scanners had spotted something awry with our hand-baggage as we prepared to board our flight. The offending article turned out to be an umbrella. Strange things, umbrellas! They obscure your line of vision. They threaten to poke your eyes out. Given a fair wind they are even fairly well disposed to turning themselves inside out. You would be daft to use one in a plane, but I suppose they could conceal a dangerous weapon, or a spring release might detonate something. It's always best to be on the safe side. Our lives might hang in the balance, after all.

The church we went to in Sydney had a permanent display of brightly coloured and open umbrellas hanging from the glass roof of the open-air portico that ran along its outer wall. It's all part of the Umbrella Project. These umbrellas 'hang around' as a reminder of the shade and shelter that the church and other organizations try to bring to the rising number of homeless people in the city. Their lives are in the balance, too.

The parable of Jonah in the Old Testament sees Jonah sheltering at the end under the shade of a bush. You might call that bush nature's umbrella. He was annoyed when the bush died and he couldn't get any shelter any more. God told him off for being obsessed with his own needs rather than those of the city he had told him to preach to. Jonah played it safe. That's always a big temptation. I think God wants us to know that there's more to life than our own security.

Jesus acting without regard for his own safety . . .

When Jesus came down from the mountainside, large crowds followed him. A man with leprosy came and knelt before him and said, 'Lord, if you are willing, you can make me clean.' Jesus reached out his hand and touched the man. 'I am willing,' he said. 'Be clean!' Immediately he was cleansed of his leprosy.

Matthew 8: 1–3

A prayer

Lord, a nice brightly coloured umbrella might have been very useful to you. People could have spotted you from miles away. But then, you would probably have opened it up at the most inappropriate times. You managed to get enough people annoyed, even without one. Amen

Vietnamese lessons

'You won't get much out of my father, you know. His English isn't that good.' We were on our way to see Rachael's prospective in-laws. Rachael and Tam had recently got engaged and were taking us to meet them. They were originally from Vietnam and had made a successful life as market gardeners in Australia. There was going to be a small engagement party with a few friends and family.

It seemed like a fair proportion of the Vietnamese community of Western Australia turned up to that party. We enjoyed Vietnamese karaoke, the singing marked with a complete lack of inhibitions. They loved the microphone. The food and the wine flowed in equal abundance to the singing and laughter. It was a fantastic party.

One of the Vietnamese men came over and eventually started talking about where he had come from. Tam's father came over, too and just quietly listened. I learned how they had come over as boat people – to escape incredible hardship, fear and poverty. This man spoke of how different it was for the younger generation. 'But we want them to remember where we have come from.' And Tam's father spoke up: 'Yes, it's important that they don't forget.' We soon realized his English was a lot better than we had thought.

It wasn't that they lived in the past; they didn't. But what they had gone through gave them a distinctive perspective.

Remembering where they came from . . .

When you harvest the grapes in your vineyard, do not go over the vines again. Leave what remains for the foreigner, the fatherless and the widow. Remember that you were slaves in Egypt.

Deuteronomy 24: 21–22

A prayer

Lord, you know how it is. You just get on with life as it is and it is easy to forget how you came to challenge people, change their lives, and see God from a new perspective. I just wanted to say thank you for those who remind us what this thing we call salvation is about – and how much it cost. I think that calls for a celebration. Amen

Ask the Waldecks

The shape that loomed in the distance of an otherwise featureless road was a church. Whatever other buildings had once befriended it had long since disappeared. We turned the car round the corner and pulled up. The church window was covered in plastic sheeting and its last service must have been many years ago. The National Trust sign said the Wesley Church was built by convict labour and opened in 1870. The early settlers were members of a strong Wesleyan community led by the Waldecks who lived at nearby Mt Pleasant.

My sense of their strong faith in an unforgiving environment was only heightened when I returned to the car. We had parked next to a home-made notice by the roadside on which someone had daubed: *Caution. Pythons crossing. Slow. Harmless. Protected species.* I got back in the car quickly, wondering if the Waldecks had somehow inadvertently assisted the survival of the python population.

Maybe the Waldecks simply moved on. I don't know. The pythons have remained though. Unlike them, we Christians are not a protected species. No-one is going to stick a sign up to preserve us. We are engaged in the mission of Christ sometimes in unforgiving environments. But then so was Jesus himself. None of us can afford to be complacent when it comes to mission. Ask the Waldecks.

In the presence of God and of Christ Jesus, who will judge the living and the dead, and in view of his appearing and his kingdom, I give you this charge: Preach the word; be prepared in season and out of season; correct, rebuke and encourage – with great patience and careful instruction.

2 Timothy 4: 1–2

A prayer

Lord, I see why you chose Paul. He certainly knew how to motivate young Timothy. You did not ask him to talk about options, possibilities, dreams or responsibilities. You asked Paul to give Timothy a charge! It makes me wonder what charge you have now given me. Amen

The town of Berry

There is a small township in New South Wales that rejoices in the very endearing and charming name of *Berry*. One of its many attractions is a signpost containing over 60 signs pointing you in the direction of places near and far. They included places I'd heard of: The Sahara Desert (16,224 km), Gdansk (15,725 km) and Bethlehem (3,815 km); places I might like to visit: Lord Howe Island (7,999 km) or the Berry Donut Van (1 minute); and places that don't even exist. I had to look up Waikikamukau (pronounced Whykickamoocow) only to discover it is a generic name for any small rural town in New Zealand! The distance there was identified simply as '?'.

I remembered Jesus once told a scribe he was not far from the kingdom of God. I suppose I am something of a scribe myself and I wondered how far this other Berry was from the kingdom, too. Would you measure that distance in kilometres, minutes or question marks? The scribe whom Jesus addressed certainly knew his priorities. He could talk about loving God with all his heart, soul, mind and strength and loving his neighbour as himself. The question really, I suppose, was: what was he going to do about that? He was not far from the kingdom. You and I might think the signs were not really that good. But actually Jesus sounded remarkably hopeful about him.

How far are you from the kingdom of God? It's a Berry sort of question. Maybe we should just settle for the signs that point us in the right direction. Or better still, we follow the signs and actively build the kingdom.

The scribe

'To love him [God] with all your heart, with all your understanding and with all your strength, and to love your neighbour as yourself is more important than all burnt offerings and sacrifices.' When Jesus saw that he had answered wisely, he said to him, 'You are not far from the kingdom of God.'

Mark 12: 33–34

A prayer

Lord, I reckon that there must be times when I am thousands of miles away from the kingdom. That Donut Van can sound a lot more enticing. I am amazed you never cease to hope in the likes of us. When you are pointing me in the right direction help me to recognize the signs and take the right road. Amen

Sydney Observatory

We arrived at the Sydney Observatory at 12.30 pm. As Observatories go, it is fairly modest and not a patch on Greenwich but it did have one unusual feature. On top of the tower is a distinctive and fairly large yellow ball. At a few minutes before 1.00 pm every day this ball 'climbs' to the top of the mast and at the exact moment that 1.00 pm is reached it miraculously drops to the bottom of the mast again.

The original purpose of course was not to entertain visiting 'anorak poms', but to signal the exact time to passing ships, which was essential if they were to navigate successfully.

There is a sense in which our churches, chapels, Christian communities function as Observatories. We focus our lenses not so much on the stars, but on our Father who is in heaven. We observe what he was doing in and through Jesus; we talk about it with one another and we try and make sense of that today. Of course if we then don't tell ourselves and others the right time – whether now is the right time to change, to love, to believe in God (and ourselves), to seek justice or reconciliation, to step out in faith, to be healed or to be patient – then we become simply redundant.

If you really feel the need to construct a mast and yellow ball on your church, then go ahead; just remember Jesus died at 3.00 pm, not 1.00 pm. But maybe God would be happier if we just took him into account when we ask what time it really is – and navigate accordingly.

'The time has come,' Jesus said. 'The kingdom of God has come near. Repent and believe the good news!'

Mark 1: 15

Then he returned to the disciples and said to them, 'Are you still sleeping and resting? Look, the hour has come, and the Son of Man is delivered into the hands of sinners.'

Matthew 26: 45

A prayer

Lord, don't you think you might have let your disciples have another couple of hours' sleep? And why is it that when I think it is time for one thing you tell me it is time for something else? Just give me a minute while I reset my watch to your time. Amen

Slipper Orchid Christians

At first sight the most startling things to be found in the wet tingle forests are the Red Tingles, huge trees that grow up to 75 m in height and 20 m in girth. They are quite simply vast. But the forests are home to much smaller but equally fascinating forces of nature. The tingle forest is the ideal habitat for a variety of orchids, and of these there is just one that actually grows on trees.

It's called the Slipper Orchid (*Cryptiostylis ovata*, if you are into Latin) and it is a beautiful red and green flower. It produces a scent that male wasps find irresistible and that is because its scent is remarkably similar to that produced by female wasps. So you have unsuspecting male wasps moving from orchid to orchid looking for a mate and spreading pollen between the flowers as they go, while no doubt female wasps look down with a mixture of bewilderment, bemusement, and whatever the buzz is for 'I told you so!' Now that is one very clever, ingenious orchid.

Maybe you are more of a Slipper Orchid Christian than a Red Tingle Christian. God has placed you in a unique situation. In many respects, even though you think no-one notices you apart from God, you are unique, too. Maybe you are the only Christian in your home, your street, your office. That makes you a missionary. Leave the muscular stuff to the Red Tingles, if you like, but you can develop your own cryptic style. And don't hesitate to be ingenious. It could be the new buzz word.

From the Parable of the Dishonest Steward

And his master commended the dishonest steward because he had acted shrewdly.

Luke 16: 8

A prayer

Lord, it's all very well putting me in unique situations, and telling me to be shrewd and ingenious, but when is the training course? And what do you do if you are not irresistible? All I can do is use my eyes and ears, pray for people, and trust you to be my guide. Don't let me down. Amen

Producing good wine

Not too far from the heart of the wine country in south-western Australia lies a small town called Cowaramup. It's not easy even for locals to pronounce, so it's commonly called Cowtown and local entrepreneurs have cashed in and produced life-sized replicas of cows all over the town. They were introduced to the public in July 2012 on International Cow Appreciation Day. The annual festival to celebrate this is called, rather sadly, Deja Moo.

Now while I have nothing against cows, or entrepreneurs for that matter, it left me feeling slightly uneasy. Especially when I learned that Cowaramup has nothing to do with cows. It's an aboriginal name meaning 'the place of the cowara', or as we would say, the purple-crowned lorikeet – a rather striking bird of many colours. And 'place of the cowara' is perhaps more distinguished than the early settlers' name for the earlier settlement, which was Group 12 Campsite.

Christian faith exists because of the Group of 12 that believed Jesus had been raised. We have moved on a lot since those days. Times have changed beyond all recognition. It's important that we do change and adapt, but in ways that reflect and enhance what it is we are all about as Christians. Whether our style is traditional or modern, it is important that our style should never rule over our substance. I'd like to think the cowara not only look good but actually sing a distinctive tune.

From Paul to Timothy

What you heard from me, keep as the pattern of sound teaching, with faith and love in Christ Jesus. Guard the good deposit that was entrusted to you – guard it with the help of the Holy Spirit who lives in us.

2 Timothy 1: 13–14

A prayer

Lord, help us to live in such a way that we produce a really good wine. Amen

For God's sake

Her favourite phrase was 'for God's sake' and she would repeat it several times a day. When something annoyed her; if she was interrupted; if someone said anything that even mildly disturbed her you knew what was coming: 'for God's sake.' I don't think she even knew how frequently she said it and when someone suggested, tongue-in-cheek, that she might like to try an alternative like 'for crying out loud' her response was: *For God's sake, don't be so ridiculous!*

The irony of it all of course was that God had nothing at all to do with it. Restoring the gentle equilibrium and pattern of her life was not for God's sake. It was for hers. I often wondered how she would have responded if someone had suggested that, after all these years of invoking his name, now really was the time to do something for God's sake.

Every so often God will visit your church. I am not suggesting he hasn't been before, but this time it's special. He will offer you a gift. Now this gift might come in the form of a person, an opportunity, a letter, a dream or even a legacy. Accepting the gift might be easy or it may be hard. It might involve changes or sacrifices that sit uncomfortably with you and you might well be inclined to say 'For God's sake!'

But when God visits you with this gift, be under no illusions; it is for a reason. It could be for your benefit or it could be for others. It might indeed not be what seems right to you. It might even involve a huge level of sacrifice. But that gift might just prove to be a godsend in all sorts of ways, so when it comes for God's sake, accept it.

From the Sermon on the Mount

Which of you, if your son asks for bread, will give him a stone? Or if he asks for a fish, will give him a snake? If you, then, though you are evil, know how to give good gifts to your children, how much more will your Father in heaven give good gifts to those who ask him!

Matthew 7: 9–11

A prayer

Lord, have you really taken on board how hard it is to do things for your sake? I don't think I should have asked you that, should I? A fleeting image of Jesus in the Garden of Gethsemane just came to mind. Not my will, but thine. I think I am going to need a bit of help on that one. Amen

Geraldton War Memorial

One of the most compelling statues I have ever seen is to be found at a War Memorial at Geraldton in Western Australia. The site was built to commemorate and honour the 645 Australian sailors who were lost off the Western Australian coast during a World War II battle with a German raider in November 1941. Both ships were lost, though many of the German crew survived. All on the Australian cruiser HMAS Sydney II lost their lives.

You can see a silver dome of 645 seagulls which represent each of the lost Sydney sailors. The wall of remembrance shows you photographs of the ship and the names of the Sydney crew. But it is the bronze statue of a woman, her hand holding her hat down on her head in the face of the oncoming wind and gazing desperately out to sea that cuts you to the quick. Fear, anxiety and longing are etched into her face as she waits news of the missing ship. You feel there is nothing she would not do to bring her husband or son home. She almost looks alive. And it made me realise how important longing is when we remember.

Today we shall stop for a minute or two to remember those who lost their lives in war. We shall remember those who risk their lives in conflicts today – men, women and children. It can be overwhelming. But longing for a different world, longing for peace, longing for what sometimes might seem impossible stops us who are alive from becoming statues.

From the Psalms

As a deer longs for flowing streams,
so my souls longs for you, O God.

Psalm 42: 1

From John's Gospel

Peace I leave with you; my peace I give you. I do not give to you as the world gives. Do not let your hearts be troubled and do not be afraid.

John 14: 27

A prayer

Lord, sometimes statues do seem alive. You almost think they are real and can touch them. It seems odd to think that we can become statues ourselves, rooted to the spot and unable to move. Lord as I remember today, as I remember people's sacrifices and as I remember yours, instil in me a deeper longing for life and for you. Amen

The pioneering spirit

One of the things I have never done is parachuting. I am not very good with heights so it might not be a good idea. Not that I have any doubts about its safety. After all, people have been parachuting for years – 216 years to be precise. The first parachutist was a Frenchman called André-Jacques Garnerin. He was taken up by a balloon, and went up to 3,000 feet in a basket, to which his parachute was attached. Garnerin cut the rope, the balloon carried on up, the parachute opened and Garnerin floated down, though not exactly gently.

A couple of years later, he took a woman up with him, but not before being summoned to the Police who had been advised that reduced air pressure might affect the delicate organs of a woman. More importantly there was the moral question of whether it was seemly for a man and a woman to share the same basket without a chaperone!

The stories of Jesus might seem as familiar to us as the notion of parachuting, but it's worth remembering just how much Jesus was at the cutting edge of dealing with people (especially women), the authorities and indeed God. There would have been many who would have seen him as every bit as daft as the celebrated Frenchman. He encouraged people to join him in taking a leap of faith, albeit of a different kind. So when you read or hear of what Jesus was up to, just remember that what you are hearing was pioneering stuff.

I still have no intentions to go parachuting, though.

Jesus is anointed by a sinful woman

When the Pharisee who had invited him saw this, he said to himself, 'If this man were a prophet, he would know who is touching him and what kind of woman she is – that she is a sinner.' Jesus answered him, 'Simon, I have something to tell you.'

'Tell me, teacher,' he said.

'Two people owed money to a certain moneylender. One owed him five hundred denarii, and the other fifty. Neither of them had the money to pay him back, so he forgave the debts of both. Now which of them will love him more?'

Luke 7: 39–42

A prayer

Lord, leaps of faith are all very well and interesting till you start asking us to take them ourselves. Are you aware that we might get hurt? Amen

The prince at Mow Cop

I baptized a baby boy recently and in the course of the service the mother referred to her son as her little prince. Now you might be forgiven for thinking that I was standing in for the Archbishop of Canterbury at the christening of Prince George, but no, this was actually at Mow Cop. I remember once reading of a poor black American who had come to faith in Christ. *I am now a prince because I am the child of Christ the King,* he said. And he was absolutely right. And so was the young Mum at Mow Cop.

Now I mention this because today is sometimes called the Feast of Christ the King. As feasts go it is relatively new, and it was inaugurated by the Pope Pius XI in 1925. Europe was changing and dictatorships were on the rise, which would have catastrophic effects upon the whole world. The influence of the church on ordinary people was also waning fast.

The Feast of Christ the King reminded people that Christ was a different kind of King. It challenged everyone to think who and what was the ultimate authority in their lives. How you answered that challenge was more than simply a theoretical exercise; it was a matter, quite literally in some cases, of life and death. To say that Christ is our king is no small matter even today. The implications are enormous and yet endearingly joyful.

A question of kingship

[Pilate said to Jesus:] *'Are you the King of the Jews?' . . . Jesus answered, 'My kingdom does not belong to this world. If my kingdom did belong to this world, my attendants would be fighting to keep me from being handed over to the Jews. But as it is, my kingdom is not here.' So Pilate said to him, 'Then you are a king?' Jesus answered, 'You say I am a king. For this I was born and for this I came into the world, to testify to the truth.'*

John 18: 33b, 36–37

A prayer

Lord, you know as well as I do all the different claims others make on my life. Not to mention the other priorities that draw me, too. But, as the hymn goes, you are my king and I will extol you. There you are, I have said it, and what is more, I believe it. Amen

Like choice morsels

Welcome to Advent, as we prepare for the birth of the 'Word made flesh'. Words communicate, so this month's letters are about communication – God's and ours.

You don't have to be a fan of Les Dawson's Cissie and Ada to understand gossip. People do gossip – even in the church – and the effects can be both insidious and destructive. You might be surprised to know, though, that gossip had a quite different meaning in the Middle Ages. A gossip was a child's godmother or godfather. 'Gossip' is short for 'god-sib', which is itself an abbreviated form of 'god sibling'. Thus, your gossips were the women and men you chose as godparents for your child – they were your brothers and sisters in Christ. They nurtured you in your faith. Those are the kind of gossips we want.

The Christmas story tells us about people who would in the normal course of events have been the subject, or victim, of other people's gossip. There is Mary, carrying a child, and the man to whom she is betrothed is not the father. There were shepherds in the fields, not exactly renowned for their manners, reliability, or religious observance. Then there were visitors from the east – foreigners. Enough said! They were all fair game for a village tongue-lashing. But, as the scene is set for the birth of Jesus, God calls them to play significant roles in a remarkable story. As Mary put it, from now on all generations will call me blessed.

Don't gossip, in the modern sense of the word. Don't speak ill of others or diminish what they offer. Be an old-fashioned kind of gossip. Spread the good news around. Be a godparent to others and nurture them in the faith. It's good communication.

One of the Proverbs

The words of a gossip are like choice morsels; they go down to the inmost parts.

Proverbs 18: 8

Prayer

Yes, Lord, a bit of gossip can be very tasty, but I know where this is leading. I ask your forgiveness for when I have spoken without love, when I have listened to gossip and not stopped it in its tracks. And I pray for those who have been hurt by whispers and back-biting. We all love a good story – but you invite us to enter a life-changing one. Amen

The art of an insult

Groucho Marx once said: *I've had a perfectly wonderful evening – but this wasn't it.* Well, we all enjoy a good insult, just so long as it is not directed at us. Maybe today you will hear the story of John the Baptist. He was quite good at insults. There he is in the desert, with people coming from all over to see him and along come some Pharisees and Sadducees. *You brood of vipers,* he calls them. Or, more literally, *you offspring of snakes.* Now having your parentage called into question doesn't go down too well at the best of times, but in a culture where snakes are about as low as you can get, this was an insult of epic proportions.

Now it may be that John was simply an awfully rude young man, but there was actually a point to this. John believed God was about to do something radically new. [In Jesus, as it turned out.] The world was going to be a significantly different place when his kingdom comes. That's now just round the corner and we should get ready for it by repenting. That meant changing your tack, your priorities, your behaviour. Where did the Pharisees go wrong? They thought that repentance might apply to a lot of other people but it didn't actually apply to them. They didn't need to change. Now this was a bit like a red rag to a bull as far as John was concerned. Indeed it was a lot more offensive – to God as much as anyone else – than any insult he might offer.

Thank you, Philip, that was just what they needed to hear, someone said after one of my services. Maybe one day he will have a perfectly wonderful evening and know that God was actually speaking to him – but this wasn't it.

John prepares the way of the Lord

In those days John the Baptist came, preaching in the wilderness of Judea and saying, 'Repent, for the kingdom of heaven has come near.' This is he who was spoken of through the prophet Isaiah:

'A voice of one calling in the wilderness,

'Prepare the way for the Lord, make straight paths for him.'

Matthew 3: 1–3

A prayer

Lord, forgive me if I sometimes think Christmas is really for the children or just someone else. Do you know how hard it is to believe that what you give is actually for me? Lord, prepare the way in the stony ground of my heart. Amen

An intense prayer

There is a school in Congleton called *Daven.* It is an interesting name. Since Davenport, one of my churches, means 'gateway to the Dane', I can only assume that Daven somehow derives its meaning from the River Dane, too.

But *daven* also has another meaning. In traditional Jewish worship people don't just 'pray' or 'read prayers'; they daven. If you have ever seen pictures of Jewish men or women at prayer they sing, chant, move and sway as they pray. There is an emotional intensity in what they are doing. It's as if their whole selves are involved in saying their prayers, not just their minds, their hearts or their lips. That is what it means to *daven.*

Sometime this Advent you may hear or sing The Magnificat, that wonderful song of Mary when she is almost overwhelmed by the recognition that she is to bear a child and that God has chosen her. To understand the intensity of that prayer, maybe we have to imagine Mary not standing still, but rocking, swaying even dancing as she sings her heart out.

Perhaps that unfamiliar word can give us a hint of how Mary sang her song. She is being drawn into the passionate love of God for his people that results in the giving of his own Son to be born at Bethlehem. And if we can sing that song with something of that raw emotional intensity, then we can only expect to be drawn in ourselves. *Love divine, all loves excelling.* Or should that be *Love daven*?

Mary's Song

And Mary said: 'My soul magnifies the Lord and my spirit rejoices in God my Saviour, for he has been mindful of the humble state of his servant. From now on all generations will call me blessed, for the Mighty One has done great things for me – holy is his name.'

Luke 1: 46–49

A Prayer

Lord, whether I am still, or whether I am restless; whether I am quiet, or whether I am noisy, help me to grasp the measure of your love and grace in Jesus. And having grasped it, help me to enjoy it. Amen

A powerful declaration

The Declaration of Independence was adopted by the Continental Congress on 4 July 1776, when 13 American colonies, then at war with Great Britain, regarded themselves as independent states, and no longer a part of the British Empire.

When Mary fell pregnant the most natural thing in the world would have been for Joseph to issue his own declaration of independence. He would 'divorce' Mary and let society take whatever revenge or decision they thought fit against her. Joseph decided not to do that. Instead he listened to the voice he had heard in a dream and supported Mary. Then in one of the most powerful yet deceptively simple declarations anywhere in the Bible, Joseph named the baby Jesus.

It may not sound a powerful declaration, but it was. People have often wondered how they should refer to Joseph. Is he a step-father or an adoptive father? How is his role to be understood? From the moment Joseph names Jesus he becomes in legal terms Jesus' father. [The assumption was you would not acknowledge any child that was not your own.] And that, in Jesus' day, was all that counted. As far as the law was concerned, Joseph was in every sense Jesus' father.

Declarations are more than just words. They embody a commitment to a course which will often have profound repercussions. What happened in 1776 changed the course of history. Joseph's declaration that Jesus was his son saved Mary and committed him to an uncharted and different future which lay in God's hands.

The child born in a stable in Bethlehem is my Lord and Saviour. Now there is a declaration.

Joseph's Story

When Joseph woke up he did what the angel of the Lord had commanded him and took Mary home as his wife. But he did not consummate their marriage until she gave birth to a son. And he gave him the name Jesus.

Luke 1: 24–25

A Prayer

Lord, I confess I have never really noticed Joseph. He always plays second fiddle to Mary. But what I see is a strong, courageous, faithful and guiding hand. I ask you to give me something of what Joseph had as I declare my faith. Amen

The call to make things new

Over the course of this last month I have focussed on some of the ways we use words. We gossip; we insult; we speak with passion and intensity; we declare where we stand.

In John's Gospel, Jesus is spoken of as the Word made flesh. It does sound rather an odd way to talk about anybody. It really means: here was a man who spoke for God in a unique way. And in spite of, or perhaps because of, that people gossiped about him. Rumours of what he had said and done travelled wide, and the spin on it was not always positive. Jesus was insulted, the victim of cruel words, even when he was being crucified. Yet he had shown his Father's love not just in words or actions but also with an extraordinary degree of passion. And right to the very end he never ceased to declare his faith in God.

But those words from John also point to something else. They deliberately echo the opening words of the Bible from Genesis. The Lord spoke and there was light, and life. God's words created something new. And now Jesus was speaking, *the* Word, and something new was happening all over again. Water would be changed into wine. Men and women will be fed in their thousands. Ordinary people will find a Good Shepherd. And though others may try, this creative force of love will not be stopped.

Even when we are gossiped about, when we are insulted, when our passion deserts us, or when the declarations of faith and intent we once made have diminished in their intensity, there is still a Word that says *Come unto me. I can make all things new.* Jesus is the Word that continues to have the power to renew our lives and reshape our world.

The experience of a suffering church

And he that sat upon the throne said, Behold, I make all things new. And he said unto me, Write: for these words are true and faithful.

Revelation 21: 5

A Prayer

Lord, I want to thank you for the gift of speech, for conversations and stories, letters and books. Please guide me in how I speak, because the words don't always come out right. Maybe, as the living Word, you can do something new with them. Amen

Ready at five-to-six

It was 1755 when John Wesley first introduced people to the Covenant Service. Those who are accustomed to a 24-hour clock may think that thrusting it upon an unsuspecting congregation at five-to-six sounds a little hasty and ill-thought out. But I strongly suspect that he had been working at it for some time.

To my reckoning, we have been making our Covenant promises for 258 years. The service is one of the jewels in the Methodist Crown but that doesn't make it popular. Some people make a point of avoiding it. Why? Probably because they don't like making promises they can't keep. Or they don't like coming to church and finding themselves suddenly confronted with a service of such magnitude they are not ready for. *Nobody told me it was Covenant Service today!* Or they just think it is very old hat.

The problem is we get this jewel out of its box once a year, look quizzically at those who admire its sparkle, and then put it back again. Which is not at all how John Wesley imagined it. He expected people to go to a series of meetings first. There would be sermons, classes and guidelines to take onboard. You would be encouraged to take a day out preparing yourself by fasting, prayer and self-examination. And by the time you got to five-to-six that night you would be ready. After it was all over you would then have to work out how you were going to keep your promises.

So it might seem rather odd to have the Covenant Service so early in the year when we don't have time to prepare for it properly. Maybe the experience of Christmas and New Year in 1755 was rather different then. This year try to resist the temptation to put the jewel back in its box at five-to-seven.

A fresh perspective

'The command that I am giving you today is not too difficult or beyond your reach. It is not up in the sky . . . Nor is it on the other side of the ocean . . .'

Deuteronomy 30: 11–13

A Prayer

Lord, thanks at least for the five-minute warning. Mind you, I am not sure I will ever really be ready for the promises your love warrants in return. Do you never feel that your relationship with me is a bit one-sided? Renew a right spirit within me Lord. Amen

When you can't keep the promises

In the beginning, God . . . That's how Genesis begins. You are left with no doubt as to who this book is about. I suspect that John Wesley encouraged Christians to participate in the Covenant Service at the beginning of the year because he wanted them to remember the big picture. This is about God.

You might be forgiven for thinking that actually the Covenant Service is about us. *The central part of that Service is surely the promises we make.* Well they are certainly very important but the heart of it is God. The Covenant is a special relationship between us and God, and that it exists at all is because it is a gift of God to us. When God gave us life he did not ask us first. When he gave us a new beginning through Jesus he did not ask us first.

He just did it – because that is the kind of God he is. One who creates new beginnings at extraordinary cost to himself. You and I do not deserve that special relationship. We don't deserve forgiveness or even to have God listen to us. The Covenant is neither a burden nor an award. It's a way of life we enter into where God and his love are central.

There is no doubt that the Covenant Promises are demanding and extraordinary, even for the most extraordinary of saints. But if you have to steel yourself to make them you have missed the point. They are simply the natural response to what we have experienced, learned and shared of God's amazing grace. What do we do if we can't keep those promises? We celebrate a God who forgives us and who keeps his promises. It's really about God, you know. He's much bigger than you might think.

The initiative is God's

'The days are coming,' declares the Lord, 'when I will make a new covenant with the people of Israel and with the people of Judah.'

Jeremiah 31: 31

A Prayer

Lord, today when I made my promises, I thought I was asking a lot of myself. Then it felt as if my words were simply echoes of the promises you have made to me. And I felt the enormity of your presence. And I knew I was in the right place at the right time. I felt you were beginning something new again and wanted me to be a part of it. Only not just me; us together. Your people. Amen

Oh golly, Miss Molly!

Oh golly, Miss Molly! Or Mrs Molly in John Wesley's case. In 1751 he married Mary (Molly) Vazeille, a well-to-do widow and mother of four children. Things started going downhill after three months and by 1758 she had left him – unable to cope, it is said, with the competition for the time and devotion the ever-burgeoning Methodist movement seemed to demand. Molly returned and left him again on several occasions before they finally split up permanently.

Despite their rather dysfunctional relationship, Wesley saw the Covenant as very much a kind of marriage – between us and God. He probably thought it would work out rather better. His original Covenant Prayer involved taking Christ as 'my Head and Husband, for better, for worse, for richer, for poorer, for all times and conditions, to love, honour and obey thee before all others, and this to the death'. If Molly ever said *I hope you treat God then much better than you treat me* you might entertain some sympathy for her.

It's easy in any relationship to take someone for granted. The Covenant Service gives us an opportunity to celebrate our relationship with God; or you may prefer to speak in terms of your relationship with Jesus. At the beginning of the year it also invites us to be open as to how that relationship can grow and be renewed. I don't suppose God enjoys being taken for granted any more than Molly did. Golly!

From St Paul

Love must be sincere. Hate what is evil; cling to what is good. Be devoted to one another in love. Honour one another above yourselves. Never be lacking in zeal, but keep your spiritual fervour, serving the Lord. Be joyful in hope, patient in affliction, faithful in prayer. Share with the Lord's people who are in need. Practise hospitality.

Romans 12: 9–13

A Prayer

Lord, please understand if this is a somewhat cautious prayer. I want to be numbered as one of your disciples. I want to be faithful. I want to know you more dearly, follow you more nearly, love you more dearly and all that. However, when it comes to *before all others,* it's often those who are closest who get left out. I am hoping that one of the fruits of my covenant with you is wisdom. Amen

Open to God

This year I have had to listen, think and pray hard to discern my future in ministry. Where does God want me to be? Where I am? That would certainly have suited me, but was it where God was leading me? I asked about being a Minister in Australia – but they already have too many! I was close enough to getting a fascinating post in Europe. Every door closed. Surely God would want me to use my experience as a Superintendent! Originally I asked to be posted within an hour of Manchester. But nothing I happened to look at seemed right. But then I was not looking in the right places.

Part of the Covenant Prayer goes: *Let me be employed for you or laid aside for you.* In one sense it was only when I had got to the point where I could truly pray that prayer that I was offered and accepted a new venture that did seem 'right'. And only 35 minutes away at that!

We often say the Covenant Prayer on command, as it were, but sometimes you need to pray it at the right time for you too. John Wesley did some things he may not have been too certain about at first – preaching outdoors, appointing lay preachers, ordaining Ministers – but he was open to where God was leading him. Can I invite you to look at it again at the Covenant Prayer? It involves you and me being open to God, to where he is leading us, with all the risks and uncertainties that that sometimes entails. And if you can truly be that open to new possibilities – however daunting and even unpalatable that might seem – you will discover that God is more than faithful.

Jonah resists God's plans

The word of the Lord came to Jonah son of Amittai: 'Go to the great city of Nineveh and preach against it, because its wickedness has come up before me.' But Jonah ran away from the Lord and headed for Tarshish. He went down to Joppa, where he found a ship bound for that port. After paying the fare, he went aboard and sailed for Tarshish to flee from the Lord.

Jonah 1: 1–3

A Prayer

Lord, I am all in favour of change and taking risks. I am all in favour of looking at things afresh and anew and seeing new possibilities emerge as people take genuine steps of faith. Indeed I am more than happy seeing other people do that. I just get rather twitchy when you look at me. Amen

Are you saying we haven't repented?

I heard a new word this last week: meta-cognitive. Apparently it means thinking about what you are thinking. For example: *I remembered I keep forgetting things.* These next few letters are going to be meta-scriptoral – letters about letters.

In *Revelation* John wrote to seven churches which were facing threats, suffering, even persecution. Seven in the Bible is a special number. John might just as well have said 'all'. What John says to one church might well be relevant to the others, and indeed to everyone. It's a clever way of saying *I am writing to all of you.* John's letters are certainly well worth reading, and I would encourage you to read Revelation 2–3.

The first letter was to the church in Ephesus. The city's great claim to fame was its temple to Artemis. In its magnificent grounds stood a tree to which criminals on the run could come and claim asylum. John reminded the Ephesians of another tree, a 'tree of life', to which only those who actually repented could come.

You can almost hear the Ephesians saying: *Are you saying we haven't repented?* Well John reminded them of their qualities. They were hard-working, patient, and discerning of who spoke with real Christian authority. But . . . John wanted them to remember that they kept forgetting something. They had once made love the very heart of their life, as Jesus had done. They did indeed need to repent and get back on track again.

The Letter to Ephesus

You have persevered and have endured hardships for my name, and have not grown weary. Yet I hold this against you: you have forsaken the love you had at first. Consider how far you have fallen! Repent and do the things you did at first.

Revelation 2: 3–5

A Prayer

Lord, John didn't mince his words, did he? I want to take this moment to come to your tree, the Cross, to remember I keep forgetting things. Forgive me when I have become complacent. Forgive me when I have relegated your love, for me and others, to second or third fiddle. Time to get back on track, Lord, sovereign Lord. Amen

Living under threat

In December 2013, news emerged of the kidnapping of five Orthodox nuns from a Christian village called Maaloula near Damascus. They belonged to the Orthodox Monastery of Santa Tecla when they were taken during the night. This was not the first kidnapping of Christians in Syria, but it shocked the Syrian Christian community. As far as I am aware the nuns have still not been released.

When John wrote to the Church at Smyrna, in Turkey, he was talking to people at the sharp end of Christian experience. The local synagogue appeared to be making all kinds of hostile accusations towards them. They were living in dangerous times and might even be facing martyrdom, let alone kidnapping.

John does not write from the safety of an ivory tower. He writes as a brother and partner in suffering (Revelation 1: 9). He is blunt. Christ is risen; that is where he begins. It may be no coincidence that the city of Smyrna had once been destroyed and then rebuilt. Resurrection comes in many forms. What John offered was not benign encouragement but the living Lord, and hope in God's renewing power, even if they should lose their lives.

Maaloula is a village where some of the residents still speak a version of Aramaic, which was the language Jesus predominantly spoke. John wanted the Christians in Smyrna to continue to speak and act as Jesus might have done, even when they were threatened and in a state of shock. That is no small order. When Jesus was threatened, he prayed for other people. Praying for the people of Syria might be a good start.

Letter to the church at Smyrna

Do not be afraid of what you are about to suffer.

Revelation 2: 10

A Prayer

Lord, to be a partner in someone else's suffering seems to me a calling, a challenge and a privilege. It seems strange to be praying for the people of Syria from a position of comfort and peace, but what I enjoy I would like them to enjoy too. If you would hear my prayer, may they all be released from this madness, soon. Amen

The narrow way

Pergamum was one of the great cities of the ancient world. It was a healing and therapeutic centre, and even had a hospital for the mentally ill. It had a fantastic library of over 200,000 books and it was the place where parchment was invented. And all John could mention was the dangers it presented to the church in terms of idol worship and sexual immorality! But then he wasn't interested in promoting tourism. He wanted a church that knew what it was about and that would not sell out to the prevailing culture of the time.

In World War II, Dietrich Bonhoeffer had to decide how, as a Christian, he was going to stand up to Hitler. Ultimately he was arrested and was executed. He once wrote: *There remains for us only the very narrow way, often extremely difficult to find, of living every day as if it were our last, and yet living in faith and responsibility as though there were to be a great future.*

He could have caved in. He fell in love and became engaged to an 18–year-old called Maria von Wedemeyer. But there were some things even more important than his personal happiness. John admired the Christians at Pergamum but drew the line at their capacity to do 'what everyone else was doing'. He promised that those who could conquer that particular weakness would find an intimacy with God much more rewarding than anything Pergamum could offer. And even, no doubt, what the delightful Miss Maria could offer.

Letter to the Church at Pergamum

Whoever has ears, let them hear what the Spirit says to the churches.

Revelation 2: 17

A Prayer

Lord, we there are times when we have to learn from the culture around us, and times when we have to say our faith leads us in a different direction. Help us to live in such a way that we are more likely to change the world around us in the name of Christ, than be changed by the world, to the detriment of our Christian calling. Amen

When God is a tiger

I recently visited someone who happened to have a number of cards on her window-sill. Most of them were pictures of rather endearing and cuddly kittens. If you are ever tempted to think of God as perpetually soft and playful, then read John's letter to the church in Thyatira [Revelation 2: 18–29]. This is God with attitude! More tiger than pussy cat. It makes you wonder what kind of God we present to others.

The church in Thyatira had taken tolerance just that bit too far. Pagan temples were more than just the harmless antics of a few oddballs next door. If you wanted, then, to experiment in the arts of sexual licence that would be just the place to begin. But once you start having a powerful voice in the church, in this case a woman, who is also actively associated with the temple and promoting the same things, then the purr of the pussy cat is going to give way to the roar of the tiger. I don't suppose John knew the name of the woman in question but he gave her one anyway – Jezebel! Why on earth, he is roaring, are you putting up with this?

As Christian churches, we find there are distractions enough on the outside. Maybe we have become too tolerant of those things that have crept inside that threaten to tear us apart or take us off course – jealousies, resentments, animosities of one kind or another, or misplaced priorities and allegiances. God might be unbelievably loving, but don't think for one minute he is a pushover.

Oops, just seen a tiger on the window-sill.

The letter to the church in Thyatira

I know your deeds, your love and faith, your service and perseverance, and that you are now doing more than you did at first. But . . .

Revelation 2: 19–20

A Prayer

Lord, I suppose you have to be pretty direct to get through to us sometimes. Where there are things within our own church communities we need to confront, just enable us to speak with wisdom, love, and authority. Let our witness be a sign of a new day in which love, service, faith and patience find their fulfilment in real Christian unity, hope and integrity. Amen

A butt of sack

Apparently, the Poet Laureate in this country is paid a useful salary and also gets a butt of sack (which is a barrel of sherry). Nobel Laureates just get a nice medal and 10 million Swedish Krona, but sadly they have to buy their own sherry. A laureate was originally a person crowned with a laurel wreath. When John wrote to the church at Sardis, he played pop with them, told them they were resting on their laurels, and whatever butt they had got well and truly kicked.

You see, the church at Sardis had everything going for it and their reputation was second to none. They thought they were the bees' knees. But they were living off their reputation, and the reality was they had gone to sleep, were spiritually lazy, and they needed to wake up. As I write this, I am conscious that you may be thinking: 'Philip has got such and such a church in mind.' And you are absolutely right. I am thinking of yours.

John, the writer of Revelation, was not concerned with Sardis' reputation or that of any other church. He simply wanted them to live as if Christ was returning tomorrow. He knew they were facing persecution, or at the very least difficult times ahead – and if they let slip the whole reason for their existence, that is the living Lord in their lives, they would simply not survive. Better to 'kick butt' than to drink it. That could only send you to sleep. This was a time to wake up.

The letter to the church in Sardis

I know what you have done. You have the reputation of being alive, but you are dead. Wake up! . . .

Revelation 3: 1–2

A Prayer

Lord, for the most part we are nice people, you know. We do our level best not to hurt anyone but I suppose today I ought to ask you to forgive us when we drown in the sea of our own inoffensiveness. Lord, give a cutting edge to our mission and discipleship. Amen

When God opens your door

I remember the picture very well. It was of a garden with a high wall. The sun was shining and there was a table laid out that had clearly been used for a family or friends to enjoy an afternoon basking in the warmth of a splendid English summer. But there was nobody there. Worse than that, the signs were that people had left hurriedly. A book, a magazine, a plate with a half-finished orange had been abandoned. And through the wall a large gate stood open and you could see the hazy green of the countryside in front of you.

It always intrigued me because I wondered what had happened to make these people leave so suddenly. What had called them? The church at Philadelphia would have been a small church, no more than three dozen at most. The Jewish community of several thousand would have seemed a much bigger cousin. They might feel intimidated by that. Yet John imagines this small church being approached by the risen Lord who has a key and opens a door. He invites them to go through it.

Why should we be surprised if the risen Lord is opening doors for us today? We may be small, but does God love us any the less? Those doors may be ones that have been closed a long time. Or they may represent new opportunities that open up a whole new future we never imagined before. Of course we may not be able to take everything with us, but if Jesus opens up that door, best go through it. Then, the opportunity and the challenge.

The letter to the church in Philadelphia

These are the words of the Holy One, the True One, the one who has the key of David, who opens and nobody shuts . . .

Revelation 3: 7

A Prayer

Lord, I have just discovered that Philadelphia means 'country of brotherly love'. When you open these doors for us, give us the grace to go through them together as brothers and sisters in Christ. Amen

Speaking the truth in love

If there is one thing I am an expert in, it's drinking lukewarm tea. Not that it is given to me other than piping hot, but by the time I have got even halfway down the cup I have usually been distracted by other things and the tea has gone lukewarm. It does little to enhance the taste. Of all the seven churches John writes to, the church in Laodicea is probably the one you are most likely to have heard of. And they were lukewarm. And for that they get a real pasting.

Laodicea was a centre in the banking industry, but those rich Christians needed to recognize that they were poor where it counted. Laodicea was a good place for getting eye ointment, but the Christians there are blind. Laodicea was famed for its fine black wool, but in truth the Christians were naked. Like the water that came though its streams, Laodicea was lukewarm. Enough for the Lord to spit them out of his mouth. Very harsh, but very graphic! Or should that be the other way round?

But these are not the words of an aggressive and abusive rant. These are the words of someone (the risen Lord) who counts them as his friends and simply speaks the truth in love. Then something remarkable happens. They stand in the church (his house) and he returns and knocks, still expecting his faithful servants, whom he has far from abandoned, to open the door and let him in.

The letter to the church in Laodicea

Look! I am standing here, knocking at the door. If anyone hears my voice and opens the door, I will come in and eat with them and they with me.

Revelation 3: 20

A Prayer

Lord, I wonder whether you managed it – being able to give them your withering denunciations and also reassure them you loved them. People often talk about speaking the truth in love, but being able to do so effectively and with grace is no mean feat. Not that I am asking you to stop. I'm beginning to get your drift. Amen

23rd March

Mo Farah (athletics), Sir Chris Hoy (cycling), Jason Kenny (cycling) and Sir Steve Redgrave (rowing) have won a fistful of Olympic gold medals between them – 16 to be precise. There is one other thing that they share in common. They were all born on the same day – 23rd March, which of course is today.

Does it make any difference when you are born? Well, more than you might think. There is some research that would indicate that you are more likely to succeed in sport if you are born in the first half of the school year. A youngster at the older end of his class is likely to be bigger than those who are younger. He or she is more likely to stand out, and get the best coaching and attention. According to some if you are amongst the youngest your chances of succeeding are remote. Some countries have had to face up to the reality that they may have squandered half the talents available to them.

John's Gospel tells the story of Jesus who meets a Samaritan woman at the well. She stands for all those who might usually be overlooked. He also deliberately flouts standard conventions in talking to someone who is firstly a Samaritan, secondly a woman, and thirdly a sinner. She struck gold. Maybe today, 23rd March, is a day when Jesus is asking us to bring good news to those of whom little is expected – regardless of when and indeed where they were born.

Jesus meets the woman from Samaria

Then, leaving her water jar, the woman went back to the town and said to the people, 'Come, see a man who told me everything I've ever done. Could this be the Messiah?'

John 4: 28–29

A Prayer

Lord, I bet your disciples were exasperated with you at times. You kept surprising them by doing not simply what was unexpected; you also did what some might have looked askance at. But to receive your word and your touch changed people's lives. I think we sometimes forget we are in the life-changing business. I'm glad you didn't forget. Amen

The perils of black fly

If you have problems with greenfly, just be glad you don't have black fly. The black simulium fly is an irritating little pest that breeds by river waters in Africa, bites people and in the process deposits some unpleasant little parasites that cause a variety of problems including river blindness. Some 37 million people are currently infected and yet the cost of preventing it is just a few pence for an annual dose of tablets.

The cost of giving people back their sight can be small or it can be costly. In one of the longest stories in the Gospels (John 9) Jesus heals a man born blind. The cost of the treatment is minimal – just a mixture of spittle and mud applied to the man's eyes. The man's euphoria in regaining his eyesight was not shared by everyone, especially when he indicated Jesus was the Messiah. He ended up being thrown out of the synagogue and the level of hostility to Jesus went up a notch or two. He was like a fly that need swatting.

There is usually a cost involved in getting people to see. Getting the blind to see is one thing. Getting those who think they can see but actually can't, might be more difficult. It won't cost you much to look in the mirror, open your eyes and see someone that Jesus loved, died for and rose again. It won't cost you much to look at others around you and see the same. It won't cost you much to see that witnessing to the risen Lord is primarily what we are all about. Or then again, maybe it will.

The man born blind, healed of his sight, sees something else

Jesus heard that they had thrown him out, and when he found him, he said, 'Do you believe in the Son of Man?' 'Who is he, sir?' the man asked. 'Tell me so that I may believe in him.' Jesus said, 'You have now seen him; in fact, he is the one speaking with you.' Then the man said, 'Lord, I believe,' and he worshipped him.

John 9: 35–38

A Prayer

Lord, it strikes me as ironic that a river that gives so much life can harbour such dangers. Yet you came to the water and gave something that could make all the difference. Lord, take the areas in my life to which I have become blind, rub that spittle and mud into my eyes, and let me see again. And bless all who work to give people back their sight. Amen

Ezekiel and his bones

You may have a dog that finds bones exciting. The whole prospect of finding them, chewing them, and getting the goodness out of them is enough to make any self-respecting tail wag with delight. Generally, however, we do not share the same passion for bones. Perhaps that general malaise was lifted a little when the news came that the bones of Richard III had been found, and a team of experts were able to explain the story that these bones told.

The Old Testament prophet Ezekiel got a bit excited about bones once. He had a vision of a valley full of dry bones, bleached in the sun. And when he preached to them – as normal people don't – they began to move and reconnect and live again. If you think that is strange you are not alone. Even in antiquity the rabbis told people that no man under the age of 30 should read Ezekiel's book, and women not at all.

And yet for Ezekiel these bones told a story and one completely different from the sort an archaeologist might come up with. He wanted his people, 600 years before the birth of Jesus and at a time when they were demoralized and humiliated in exile, to hear that story. They had lost hope. They had to all intents and purposes given up. These bones did not tell the story of the past. They told the story of what happens when God's Spirit blows over a scene as desolate as that. When they begin to live again, life gets exciting.

There were some equally odd people who got very excited after Jesus had been buried. They never did find his bones. And that has given us something to chew over ever since.

Ezekiel's Vision

The hand of the Lord was on me, and he brought me out by the Spirit of the Lord and set me in the middle of a valley; it was full of bones. He led me to and fro among them, and I saw a great many bones on the floor of the valley, bones that were very dry. He asked me, 'Son of man, can these bones live?'

Ezekiel 37: 1–3

A Prayer

Lord, when we talk about bones, it's usually because they ache. And when they ache they are difficult to ignore. A bit like you really. You have that habit of asking me difficult questions that go beyond my aches and pains. And Lord, the strange thing is, if I could just let go in faith, I could almost get quite excited. Amen

Collision course on Palm Sunday

Helicopters only began flying in Israel in 1951, which is a great shame. Had they been invented a couple of thousand years earlier we would have had a much clearer picture of what was going on on Palm Sunday. The bird's eye view we would have had would have revealed not one entry into Jerusalem that day, but two.

On one side of the city we would have seen Jesus riding into Jerusalem on a donkey – as Zechariah had prophesied. A number of people would have welcomed him with palm branches and enthusiastic chanting. They proclaimed him as the Messiah, the son of David. This was no bland sideshow but a carefully planned announcement that a new age and kingdom had come and with it a new king. And this king would not only bring justice and peace he would replace all the other kingdoms around.

Zooming off to the opposite end of the city we would have seen the other procession entering the city at the same time. All standard practice, it's the beginning of the Jewish Passover and in comes the Roman reminder of who is in charge. The Roman governor, Pontius Pilate, would be entering the city with soldiers, horses, banners, golden eagles on poles and all the other trappings of military might. Their banners would have proclaimed the Emperor as son of God, Lord, Saviour and bringer of peace. Well, he wouldn't be the last to have had an over-inflated opinion of himself.

What the helicopter would pick up from the air was a clear sign that there were two processions that Palm Sunday who were heading towards each other on a clear collision. This was David and Goliath all over again. Jesus was challenging a much bigger and more powerful authority. Now, on whose side am I going to land?

Palm Sunday

The disciples went and did as Jesus had instructed them. They brought the donkey and the colt and placed their cloaks on them for Jesus to sit on. A very large crowd spread their cloaks on the road, while others cut branches from the trees and spread them on the road.The crowds that went ahead of him and those that followed shouted, 'Hosanna to the Son of David!'

Matthew 21: 6–9

A Prayer

Lord, don't you think you were being just a tiny bit provocative? And on top of that you were giving ordinary people the naive hope that things might change in their lifetimes, if only they followed you and trusted you? Now you wouldn't be expecting me to think the same would you? Oh, you would. And in political matters, too? And I thought following you would be a walk in the park. Amen

There's no blueprint for Resurrection

We all respond to significant moments in our lives differently. Nowhere is that more true than in situations of great loss. Some can't believe what has happened. Others want to be busy, or look for explanations or try to find distractions. Some cope well initially but then struggle later on, while for others the opposite is true.

It's Easter Sunday and John's Gospel introduces us to three people who react very differently when they come to the empty tomb. They bring their sense of shock, grief and loss with them. Mary Magdalene is appalled, angry. The crucifixion was brutal, and now they have stolen Jesus' body. Peter doesn't know what to make of the scene he witnesses. He sees the strips of cloth left behind, but cannot process anything. He says nothing and just goes home, still numb perhaps and confused. The Beloved Disciple – probably John's thinly disguised way of referring to himself – sees the same troubling things (the empty tomb, no body, discarded wrappings) and 'saw and believed'. Now this may not mean he suddenly came to an intellectual belief in the resurrection. It may mean that what he saw encouraged him to remain faithful and loyal to Jesus, come what may. Heart and soul, he was still a follower of Jesus.

All three came to believe that Jesus was risen in their own way. There was no blueprint for this sort of thing. Mary would ultimately see beyond her tears, Peter would look beyond his sense of guilt and failure, and John would discover that what he had seen was more than wishful thinking. You can't proclaim an Easter faith by singing someone else's tune. You have to see things for yourself. But when you do, it's not just the empty tomb that looks different. The world changes. Alleluia!

The empty tomb

Early on the first day of the week, while it was still dark, Mary Magdalene went to the tomb and saw that the stone had been removed from the entrance. So she came running to Simon Peter and the other disciple, the one Jesus loved, and said, 'They have taken the Lord out of the tomb, and we don't know where they have put him!'

John 20: 1–2

A Prayer

Lord, when words fail, when explanations lose their force, when the wish that things could have been different melt away, there you are, the same Lord, crucified but risen and a power of love to be reckoned with. Amen

Do you understand what I have done for you?

You will know the experience. You hear a tune, a song, a jingle, even a hymn that keeps reverberating in your head all week almost with a will of its own. It's as if it won't let you go. I wonder if that sort of thing ever happened to the disciples after the Resurrection.

The last time Jesus had been with his disciples before his arrest was at the Last Supper. He was washing their feet and drying them with a towel. They were mortified. Jesus was their Master yet he was acting as their servant. They were deeply moved and yet uncomfortable with the experience. When he had finished, he asked them *Do you understand what I have done for you*? Well, this was deeply personal. Even before they felt the profound guilt that would soon envelop them, Jesus had washed them clean. I wonder if his words kept reverberating in their ears.

When Mary and Peter and John returned from the empty tomb, did they hear those words again in their ears? When the other disciples, or the other women at the empty tomb and even doubting Thomas, met with the risen Lord did they hear those words again: *Do you understand what I have done for you*? And what about those followers of Jesus on the road to Emmaus? Did they hear them too?

It all began on that Sunday morning in AD 33. God did something that went beyond eternal life or inspiration. He raised Jesus and opened up the possibility of reconciliation, love and hope that no-one could have imagined before. Between ourselves, our enemies and God himself. I still can't get those words out of my head: *Do you understand what I have done for you*?

Thomas begins to understand

A week later his disciples were in the house again, and Thomas was with them. Though the doors were locked, Jesus came and stood among them and said, 'Peace be with you!' Then he said to Thomas, 'Put your finger here; see my hands. Reach out your hand and put it into my side. Stop doubting and believe.' Thomas said to him, 'My Lord and my God!'

John 20 26–28

A Prayer

Lord, you know I understand and I don't understand. I can't get my head around the 'how' of the resurrection but I am beginning to understand that when you offered new life in that way you went beyond cosy, comforting words. You washed the feet of the disciples, you washed the feet of the world, and you washed mine. And so now we can walk in a new way, in a new power. Amen

Hey ho! Never mind!

It was a Friday when I was walking through the town, just an ordinary Friday. People were doing what they usually do, shopping, meeting people, trying to get to the bus in time. Life was going on as normal. But then it occurred to me that just a week earlier it had been Good Friday when we 'lifted up' the cross and remembered the crucifixion. And now . . . well it was almost as if it had never happened.

Was that what the authorities expected in Jerusalem on that fateful Friday? They will be scared witless by the horror of it all. They will see the sign 'King of the Jews' and realise that if we do that to 'kings', what can others expect? They then will go home, forget about things, and get on with their lives again. Within a short while things will be back to normal. Is that how the authorities thought? Quite possibly.

Luke's Gospel tells the story of the risen Lord meeting a couple of his erstwhile followers on the road to Emmaus. Their conversation reveals something fairly typical of expectations amongst poor village communities. They had looked forward with some enthusiasm to what Jesus would do as Messiah. But, with Jesus' crucifixion, it had all come to nothing. They had heard rumours he might be alive but they seemed to give them little credence. It was all *Hey ho! Never mind!* They headed back to Emmaus expecting life to return back to normal.

A couple of hours later their 'hearts were burning' and whatever normality was to become, whatever it looked like from the outside, it was a lot different from before.

The risen Lord eats with the disciples at Emmaus

When he was at the table with them, he took bread, gave thanks, broke it and began to give it to them. Then their eyes were opened and they recognized him, and he disappeared from their sight. They asked each other, 'Were not our hearts burning within us while he talked with us on the road and opened the Scriptures to us?'

Luke 24 30–32

A Prayer

Lord, I expect today will be as 'normal' as any other. Would you take my daily bread and bless it, so that this day might bring with it a taste of glory and the beat of a burning heart? Amen

Camping outdoors

There are differences of opinion as to what constitutes a good invitation. The opening hymn to one Camp Meeting was *Come, o come, thou vilest sinner.* Well that was in the early nineteenth century and I suppose the mood of the times has changed a little over the years! Perhaps there were competitions then as to who could claim to be the vilest (if now converted) sinner.

Actually inviting people to a Camp Meeting is not easy today anyway. However you phrase it, 'Camp Meeting' brings a different set of connotations, especially for the uninitiated. Different generations might envisage a host of boy scouts, or Butlins Red Coats, or representatives of the gay and lesbian movement. All I can say is, everyone is very welcome.

It could be that 'Camp' is short for *Can A Methodist Preach?* [We will find out.] Or *Circuit Activates Mission Priorities.* [We will find that out too.] But really a Camp Meeting is an outdoor celebration of Christian worship and witness. It challenges us (even if just for a short while) to be a Christian community without the trammels of buildings nor the restrictive constraints of local loyalties, and to be nothing more and nothing less than the people of God.

On 25 May, the Circuit Camp Meeting will be at Mow Cop in the field next to the church at 3.00 pm. It's at an inconvenient time, it may well rain and it's really difficult to get to, so it should be absolutely perfect. It is in such places that people (even vile ones) have had their most refreshing encounters with the living Lord. Don't miss it.

A welcome invitation

'Come to me, all you who are weary and burdened, and I will give you rest. Take my yoke upon you and learn from me, for I am gentle and humble in heart, and you will find rest for your souls. For my yoke is easy and my burden is light.'

Matthew 11: 28–30

A Prayer

Lord, I'd like to say I have accepted every invitation you have offered me, but I can't. Help me to recognize the good ones and to take them when they come, however strange they may sound. Amen

Helen's kind of justice

My sister was very bright. She took a first in zoology and the University wanted her to do further research with a view, I suspect, of having an academic career. But Helen wanted to teach the deaf. The University said she was wasting her gifts. They wanted her to do justice to her abilities. Helen's response was a question: why shouldn't deaf people have the best qualified teachers? The Bible talks about 'doing justice' too, and that often meant for those who might not always get it.

Helen taught deaf children for most of the rest of her life. 'Inspirational' is an over-hyped word, but in Helen's case that was exactly what she was. Her life was cut short by cancer and she died at the age of 48. It seemed so unjust, so unfair, though I cannot recall Helen herself ever speaking in those terms.

Justice, in the Bible, is a big thing. I don't think people were overly preoccupied with God. They did want to see justice done in all kinds of ways, to many kinds of people. But their fundamental experience of being freed from slavery led them to believe that God was passionate about justice even before they were. He was even introduced to some as 'a father of the fatherless and a defender of widows'.

Justice doesn't just happen. You have to do it, even when justice is not done to you. Jesus died quite unjustly. Easter declares that God's justice will have the final word. I think that is where Helen stood. One of the last things she said was: 'I know where I am going.'

A God of justice

Sing to God, sing in praise of his name,
extol him who rides on the clouds [*and*]
rejoice before him – his name is the Lord.
A father to the fatherless, a defender of widows,
is God in his holy dwelling.

Psalm 68: 4–5

A Prayer

Lord, when you look back you remember best I think the people who have shaped your life. As I thank you for those who have shaped mine, whose passion and love have been a source of inspiration, so I thank you that you shaped the lives of so many too, not least Jesus. Amen

Let justice roll

A smile came over Joanna's face as she concentrated on her iPad. Then a chuckle. And finally, 'Come over here and have a look at this.' Someone had posted a film clip of a precocious Japanese child singing. I put aside what I was concentrating on, went over and watched it, too. He was very, very good.

Sometimes the Psalms tell God to wake up (see Psalm 35: 23). Something is happening that isn't right. Justice is not being done and the writer wants to draw God into the situation: *Come over here and have a look at this.* Whether it is something that affects him personally or others, God needs to know about this! [He undoubtedly already does, but that is a different matter!]

The sense of urgency was often well placed. Widows, orphans, immigrants and the poor often lived at subsistence levels in those times and if famine, invasion, or even local unrest came about then they could be just days away from starvation. The reason why they want God to come and have a look is because they knew God to be a God of justice.

Our prayers of intercession are not just a few words to say about people we love or people in real need. They are a call to God to come and have a look at something maybe we have been looking at for a while or have only just noticed ourselves. And then to ask justice to roll.

An Old Testament prophet demands justice

But let justice roll on like a river,
righteousness like a never-failing stream!

Amos 5: 24

A Prayer

Lord, I suspect it's you saying to me sometimes: *Come and have a look at this.* And then you would probably want me to act with generosity, compassion, forgiveness and love. And not offer excuses or complain. Following you isn't the soft option is it? By the way, have you seen . . .? That can't be right. Amen

The wisdom in saying farewell

This last week I have said goodbye to my wisdom tooth. A cheerful voice said, 'That will be very painful' – and indeed I was quite apprehensive. However the procedure itself was not too bad. A large bruise appeared on my face and was completely painless, but it engendered a lot of sympathy, so was quite acceptable. Others were moved to recall their dental tales of woe and I thought I had escaped – for a couple of days; then the pain set in and I realized this was going to be a long goodbye.

This is the last month in which I shall be writing my letters in this Circuit. I only intended to write four and I shall end up at number 218. Perhaps I would have demonstrated more wisdom in finishing earlier, but I discovered that I enjoyed writing, and as Circuits got bigger and the opportunities less to visit all the congregations it has been, for me at least, a useful if one-sided way of keeping in touch.

There is a wisdom in saying goodbye. It can sometimes take a bit longer than saying hello. The bruises you see may not actually be the spots where there is hurt, and I suspect there will be moments when Joanna and I have moved on where we think we are settling well into our new home and Circuit only to discover how much we shall be missing those people and places who have played such an important part in our lives for a long time.

Thankfully there is quite a lot of stuff in the Bible about farewells. Not least in how Jesus said goodbye to people. All things considered, I think wisdom is best imparted than extracted.

A farewell blessing

The Lord bless you and keep you; the Lord make his face to shine upon you and be gracious to you; the Lord lift up his countenance upon you and give you peace.

Numbers 6: 24–26

A Prayer

Lord, at the moment when we say goodbye, you are there. You bless, you keep, you give hope, you help us see new possibilities. You give us peace. When the moments are long, may your blessing remain long with us, too. Amen

Pavilioned in splendour

It was all rather bemusing at the time. My head teacher was retiring. He stood on the cricket pavilion from where the school assembly was usually conducted; he gave a long convoluted speech, mainly about himself. It was as if the past 25 years had just flown past his mind, and then he strode off across the cricket field, his black gown flailing in the wind, his mortar board in one hand and his loyal and probably long-suffering sister on his other arm. He was always a remote and isolated figure, but I realise now that the school had been his life. It may not have been important for me to say goodbye, but it was for him. At least he left pavilioned in splendour and girded with praise.

When Jesus said goodbye, it was not for his benefit, but for others. He said quite a long farewell actually. It takes about five chapters in John's Gospel! But his goodbye begins with actions rather than words. He washes the disciples' feet. If you were going to wash feet normally you would do that before a meal, but this comes later. You know instinctively that this has nothing to do with unpleasant smells he cannot stand any longer. Feet carried you places. Judas' would take him to the place of betrayal. Peter's feet would carry him to the point of denial. The other feet, well . . . they would simply run away. In washing their feet, Jesus forgave them.

Without that gift of forgiveness, offered in advance and anticipation, I wonder whether the disciples could possibly have coped later on. They were bemused at the time, as much as I had been at school assembly. But the gift they received would be much more valuable to them than my distant memory.

A farewell act

When he had finished washing their feet, he put on his clothes and returned to his place. 'Do you understand what I have done for you?' he asked them. 'You call me "Teacher" and "Lord", and rightly so, for that is what I am. Now that I, your Lord and Teacher, have washed your feet, you also should wash one another's feet.'

John 13: 12–14

A Prayer

Lord, can't you just say goodbye like ordinary people? I used to think that your washing the disciples' feet was about teaching us to be humble. And that's OK. I can do 'humble'. Forgiveness, though – for me, for others – is a bit tougher. But I guess you already knew that. And to walk forgiven is a great gift. Amen

Death row

Meriam Yehya Ibrahim is a strikingly attractive young woman, aged 27. As I write she has just given birth to a baby girl in a Sudanese prison. Her father was a Muslim married to a Christian and he left the family when she was six years old. She has been a practising Christian ever since, but legally she is a Muslim since children, according to Sudanese law, must follow their father's faith. Meriam has been sentenced to death for the simple reason that she won't renounce her Christian faith. The punishment has been postponed till the birth of her baby and her family is waiting for an appeal.

Being on 'death row' for your faith is shocking, but sadly hauntingly familiar. During the reign of Nero, Paul was on 'death row' in a Roman prison. He had been to prison a number of times before but this time he suspected there might only be one way out. He wrote a farewell letter to Timothy, the man who had worked with him the longest. In the New Testament it is called 2 Timothy. He begins his letter: *Paul, an apostle of Christ Jesus by the will of God, according to the promise of life that is in Christ Jesus.* I suspect Timothy already knew all that in one sense – about Paul. But did he believe it about himself? Did he believe God had called him? Did he believe the life he had been given in Christ was not an optional extra but actually non-negotiable? Paul hoped the answer would be 'yes'.

Meriam Yehya Ibrahim clearly believes her life in Christ matters enormously. When you see the pictures of Meriam with her husband Daniel on their wedding day in 2011 and imagine her with her young baby, you realise just how much this remarkable woman has to live for. Let's hope and pray she never has to write a farewell letter.

From Paul, on 'death row'

At my first defence, no one came to my support, but everyone deserted me. May it not be held against them. But the Lord stood at my side and gave me strength, so that through me the message might be fully proclaimed and all the Gentiles might hear it. And I was delivered from the lion's mouth.

2 Timothy 4: 16–17

A Prayer

Lord, how can I do anything else but pray for Meriam and her family? Her faith and courage puts me to shame. Lord, give her strength, give her your Spirit, and like you once did for Paul, deliver her from the lion's mouth. Amen

A bad break

On 4 July 1939, one of the greatest farewell speeches of all time was made. Lou Gehrig, one of baseball's 'greats' had been diagnosed with a crippling muscle disorder and been forced to retire. He began: 'Fans, for the past two weeks you have been reading about the bad break I got. Yet today I consider myself the luckiest man on the face of this earth. I have been in ballparks for 17 years and have never received anything but kindness and encouragement from you fans.' He went on to talk about the people who had contributed to this self-diagnosis of good fortune – the people he had known in baseball, the fierce opponents who had sent him a gift, the groundsmen, his mother-in-law, his parents, and his wife. It's emotive and gracious stuff.

Let me paraphrase (heavily) Jesus' farewell words in John 17: 'Father, after three remarkable years I am about to get a really bad break. Yet today I consider myself the luckiest person on the earth. I have known you and done what you asked me to do. I have had some wonderful disciples. I have had all kinds of people believe in me. Now just keep them safe. They have been great gifts to me. Let the love you have had for me live in them.' It was one of the greatest farewell prayers of all time. Shortly afterwards, Jesus was arrested.

Whenever you say goodbye or pray goodbye it helps to have the right kind of perspective.

From Jesus' farewell prayer

I have made you known to them, and will continue to make you known in order that the love you have for me may be in them and that I myself may be in them.

John 17: 26

A Prayer

Lord, I think that crucifixion counts as slightly more than a bad break! But what hits me is your lack of self-pity. When I get bad breaks, help me to have something of your kind of grace and love. Amen

Gladys in the Gallery

When I trained as a Minister the prevailing notion was that you should be able to say what you need to say within 20 minutes. Times have changed, and the opportunity to write these letters has given me the challenge of reducing that time-frame to one minute. Whether I have succeeded or not is immaterial. I have enjoyed writing my letters and have taken heart that not all the sheets have been left on the seats. There has always been one person I have thought of consistently as I have written – and that is Gladys. I was introduced to her in ministerial training college. Her full name was Gladys in the Gallery, a mythical soul who would have counted herself an ordinary Christian and who probably knew a lot more about God than she or anyone else gave her credit for. If I have ever patronized Gladys, underestimated her intelligence or Christian faith then I ask her forgiveness.

Whatever our weaknesses and foibles as Christian people and congregations, whatever our gifts and graces, whatever our age and background, I hope you will never forget that Christ lives in you as much as he does in Gladys. That is a joy, a privilege and quite a challenge. To share that can take a minute, or 20 minutes. More often it takes a lifetime of faithful service and prayer. And if I have written with Gladys in mind, it is because I have received so much from Gladys, too, and lots of people like her. Never underestimate how and through whom Christ will live and work.

This is my last letter. If you have made it this far you are probably more gracious than you thought. Thank you for listening.

From St Paul

Dear brothers and sisters, I close my letter with these last words: Be joyful. Grow to maturity. Encourage each other. Live in harmony and peace. Then the God of love and peace will be with you.

2 Corinthians 13: 11

A Prayer

Lord, it is always something of a mystery to take on board that you are risen. Maybe even more so to think that you live in us. Well, time to move on and take things further. Amen